MACMILLAN MASTER ~~GUIDES~~

GENERAL EDITOR: JAMES GIBSON

Published

JANE AUSTEN	*Emma* ~~Norman Page~~
	Sense and Sensibility Judy Simons
	Persuasion Judy Simons
	Pride and Prejudice Raymond Wilson
	Mansfield Park Richard Wirdnam
SAMUEL BECKETT	*Waiting for Godot* Jennifer Birkett
WILLIAM BLAKE	*Songs of Innocence* and *Songs of Experience* Alan Tomlinson
ROBERT BOLT	*A Man for all Seasons* Leonard Smith
EMILY BRONTË	*Wuthering Heights* Hilda D. Spear
GEOFFREY CHAUCER	*The Miller's Tale* Michael Alexander
	The Pardoner's Tale Geoffrey Lester
	The Wife of Bath's Tale Nicholas Marsh
	The Knight's Tale Anne Samson
	The Prologue to the Canterbury Tales Nigel Thomas and Richard Swan
JOSEPH CONRAD	*The Secret Agent* Andrew Mayne
CHARLES DICKENS	*Bleak House* Dennis Butts
	Great Expectations Dennis Butts
	Hard Times Norman Page
GEORGE ELIOT	*Middlemarch* Graham Handley
	Silas Marner Graham Handley
	The Mill on the Floss Helen Wheeler
HENRY FIELDING	*Joseph Andrews* Trevor Johnson
E. M. FORSTER	*Howards End* Ian Milligan
	A Passage to India Hilda D. Spear
WILLIAM GOLDING	*The Spire* Rosemary Sumner
	Lord of the Flies Raymond Wilson
OLIVER GOLDSMITH	*She Stoops to Conquer* Paul Ranger
THOMAS HARDY	*The Mayor of Casterbridge* Ray Evans
	Tess of the d'Urbervilles James Gibson
	Far from the Madding Crowd Colin Temblett-Wood
JOHN KEATS	*Selected Poems* John Garrett
PHILIP LARKIN	*The Whitsun Weddings* and *The Less Deceived* Andrew Swarbrick
D. H. LAWRENCE	*Sons and Lovers* R. P. Draper
HARPER LEE	*To Kill a Mockingbird* Jean Armstrong
GERARD MANLEY HOPKINS	*Selected Poems* R. J. C. Watt
CHRISTOPHER MARLOWE	*Doctor Faustus* David A. Male
THE METAPHYSICAL POETS	Joan van Emden

MACMILLAN MASTER GUIDES

THOMAS MIDDLETON and WILLIAM ROWLEY	*The Changeling* Tony Bromham
ARTHUR MILLER	*The Crucible* Leonard Smith *Death of a Salesman* Peter Spalding
GEORGE ORWELL	*Animal Farm* Jean Armstrong
WILLIAM SHAKESPEARE	*Richard II* Charles Barber *Hamlet* Jean Brooks *King Lear* Francis Casey *Henry V* Peter Davison *The Winter's Tale* Diana Devlin *Julius Caesar* David Elloway *Macbeth* David Elloway *Measure for Measure* Mark Lilly *Henry IV Part I* Helen Morris *Romeo and Juliet* Helen Morris *The Tempest* Kenneth Pickering *A Midsummer Night's Dream* Kenneth Pickering *Coriolanus* Gordon Williams *Antony and Cleopatra* Martin Wine
GEORGE BERNARD SHAW	*St Joan* Leonée Ormond
RICHARD SHERIDAN	*The School for Scandal* Paul Ranger *The Rivals* Jeremy Rowe
ALFRED TENNYSON	*In Memoriam* Richard Gill
ANTHONY TROLLOPE	*Barchester Towers* K. M. Newton
JOHN WEBSTER	*The White Devil* and *The Duchess of Malfi* David A. Male
VIRGINIA WOOLF	*To the Lighthouse* John Mepham *Mrs Dalloway* Julian Pattison

Forthcoming

CHARLOTTE BRONTË	*Jane Eyre* Robert Miles
JOHN BUNYAN	*The Pilgrim's Progress* Beatrice Batson
T. S. ELIOT	*Murder in the Cathedral* Paul Lapworth *Selected Poems* Andrew Swarbrick
BEN JONSON	*Volpone* Michael Stout
RUDYARD KIPLING	*Kim* Leonée Ormond
JOHN MILTON	*Comus* Tom Healy
WILLIAM SHAKESPEARE	*Othello* Tony Bromham *As You Like It* Kiernan Ryan
VIRGINIA WOOLF	*Mrs Dalloway* Julian Pattison
W. B. YEATS	*Selected Poems* Stan Smith

MACMILLAN MASTER GUIDES

BARCHESTER TOWERS

BY ANTHONY TROLLOPE

K. M. NEWTON

MACMILLAN
EDUCATION

First edition 1987

Published by
MACMILLAN EDUCATION LTD
Houndmills, Basingstoke, Hampshire RG21 2XS
and London
Companies and representatives
throughout the world

Typeset in Great Britain by
TecSet Ltd, Wallington, Surrey

Printed in Hong Kong

British Library Cataloguing in Publication Data
Newton, K. M.
Barchester Towers by Anthony Trollope.
1. Trollope, Anthony. Barchester Towers
I. Title
823'.8   PR5684.B36
ISBN 0–333–43279–7 Pbk
ISBN 0–333–43280–0 pbk export

Cover illustration: *Wiltshire* by Sir Richard Colt Hoare.
Photograph © Victoria and Albert Museum, London and by
courtesy of the Bridgeman Art Library.

CONTENTS

GENERAL EDITOR'S PREFACE

The aim of the Macmillan Master Guides is to help you to appreciate the book you are studying by providing information about it and by suggesting ways of reading and thinking about it which will lead to a fuller understanding. The section on the writer's life and background has been designed to illustrate those aspects of the writer's life which have influenced the work, and to place it in its personal and literary context. The summaries and critical commentary are of special importance in that each brief summary of the action is followed by an examination of the significant critical points. The space which might have been given to repetitive explanatory notes has been devoted to a detailed analysis of the kind of passage which might confront you in an examination. Literary criticism is concerned with both the broader aspects of the work being studied and with its detail. The ideas which meet us in reading a great work of literature, and their relevance to us today, are an essential part of our study, and our Guides look at the thought of their subject in some detail. But just as essential is the craft with which the writer has constructed his work of art, and this may be considered under several technical headings – characterisation, language, style and stagecraft, for example.

The authors of these Guides are all teachers and writers of wide experience, and they have chosen to write about books they admire and know well in the belief that they can communicate their admiration to you. But you yourself must read and know intimately the book you are studying. No one can do that for you. You should see this book as a lamp-post. Use it to shed light, not to lean against. If you know your text and know what it is saying about life, and how it says it, then you will enjoy it, and there is no better way of passing an examination in literature.

JAMES GIBSON

1 ANTHONY TROLLOPE: LIFE AND CAREER

1.1 LIFE

Anthony Trollope was one of the most prolific of English novelists. During his literary career he wrote forty-seven novels, as well as short stories and several books of non-fiction. He was born in London in 1815, the son of Thomas Anthony Trollope, a lawyer, and Frances Trollope, who was herself an extremely prolific novelist. His childhood was unhappy, mainly because his father insisted on sending him and his two brothers, Thomas Adolphus (who also became a writer) and Henry, to public school even though he lacked the means to support them adequately. This led to his being ridiculed by the other boys on account of his poverty. He attended Harrow first of all and then Winchester, but showed little scholarly ability. Though his brothers went on to Oxford and Cambridge, he failed to obtain the scholarships he required to support him at university.

In 1834 he spent a short time teaching in Brussels but through the influence of his family was able to obtain a junior clerkship at the Post Office and returned to London. He was not happy at this work until the opportunity arose to take up an appointment in Ireland, where he showed considerable ability as an administrator. This period in Ireland was the turning point in his life. He not only proved to be a success in his work with the Post Office but also started a new career as a novelist.

Trollope returned to England in 1851 to work in the south west at reorganising postal services. He spent two years doing this, and during this time conceived the idea for the Barsetshire series of novels: 'In the course of the job I visited Salisbury, and whilst wandering there one mid-summer evening round the purlieus of the cathedral I conceived the story of *The Warden* – from whence came that series of novels of which Barchester, with its bishops, dean, and archdeacon, was the central site' (*Autobiography*). He then returned to Ireland and remained there until 1859. It was while he was in

Ireland that he married, in 1844, Rose Heseltine by whom he had two sons. In 1858 he went on special assignments to Egypt and the West Indies before returning to England permanently the following year. On his return Trollope took charge of the postal district of eastern England. He was less happy, however, in his work for the Post Office than he had been in Ireland, and in 1867, well established as a novelist, he resigned. In addition to writing novels and other works, he was associated with various journals, particularly the *Cornhill Magazine*, the *Fortnightly Review*, the *Pall Mall Gazette*, and *St Paul's Magazine*. He also travelled extensively, to the United States, Australia and New Zealand, and South Africa. In 1868 he attempted to enter parliament by standing as Liberal candidate for Beverley in Yorkshire, but was defeated. He died in 1882.

1.2 LITERARY CAREER

Trollope claimed he had always intended to write novels but only found the energy and the time when he went to Ireland. He attributed his success in being able to pursue two professions simultaneously to early rising. He was wakened at 5.30 every morning and worked for three hours at his writing, so that he was finished before breakfast. His first two novels dealt with Irish subjects and were unsuccessful. He then wrote a novel about the French Revolution which was also unsuccessful. He did have a modest success, however, with the first novel in the Barsetshire series, *The Warden* (1855). His earlier novels had attempted to deal with important historical subjects – the Irish potato famine, the French Revolution – but English provincial life was a subject that appealed to readers much more. *Barchester Towers* (1857) continued the success of *The Warden*, though as yet he had achieved only moderate sales. From that point on, until the latter part of his career, he was increasingly successful and made a great deal of money, with only the occasional failure.

In his autobiography Trollope disclosed that *Barchester Towers* was written mainly on trains. Since his work required a great deal of travelling, he devised a method for writing on trains: 'I made for myself therefore a little tablet, and found after a few days' exercise that I could write as quickly in a railway carriage as I could at my desk. I worked with a pencil, and what I wrote my wife copied afterwards. In this way was composed the greater part of *Barchester Towers* and of the novel which succeeded it, and much also of others subsequent to them.' Whereas Trollope received only £9 8s 8d for *The Warden*, he obtained an advance of £100 for *Barchester Towers*. He regarded this as 'a first real step on the road to substantial success'. It should be pointed out that £100 would be worth something like £3000 at today's values.

The publisher, Longman, however, had demanded that the completed novel be submitted to a reader. Trollope rejected the reader's most drastic recommendation: that the novel be cut by a third. The reader also disliked Signora Madeline Neroni's role in the novel: 'A good deal of the progress of the tale depends upon this lady . . . The character is a great blot on the work.' Trollope, however, defended her presence: though she was 'indifferent to all moralities and decent behaviour . . . such a character may, I think, be drawn without offence if her vice be not made attractive'. But Trollope did tone down some passages which the reader found 'too warm'.

The other novels in the Barsetshire series are *Doctor Thorne* (1858); *Framley Parsonage* (1861); *The Small House at Allington* (1864); and *The Last Chronicle of Barset* (1867). The Barsetshire novels were Trollope's most popular works in his lifetime and they have retained their popularity into the twentieth century. Some recent Trollope critics have argued that the later fiction, such as the Palliser series of novels, is superior to his early work. His popularity suffered towards the end of his career and for a few decades after his death. Matters were not helped by the revelations in his autobiography about his seemingly mechanical methods of work and his preoccupation with how much money he had earned as a novelist. But after the early decades of this century his popularity revived, and he has become one of the most widely read of Victorian novelists.

Critics, however, have consistently ranked him in the second division of English novelists, though more recently the spate of critical studies of his novels suggests that this assessment may be changing. Though it may be claimed that none of his novels equals in artistic merit Thackeray's *Vanity Fair*, Dickens's *Bleak House*, or George Eliot's *Middlemarch*, a considerable number of his novels are arguably not far below these. Certainly no other English novelist was so consistently good. J. A. Sutherland, in his book *Victorian Novelists and Publishers*, argues convincingly that Trollope's apparent overproduction is not a sign of artistic inferiority or mediocrity but was Trollope's way of competing in artistic terms with his great contemporaries: 'the experience of ten books, five publishers and twelve years must have convinced Trollope that his career was not going to shape like Dickens's or Thackeray's or Charlotte Brontë's. He would not break on the world with a *Pickwick* or a *Vanity Fair*. But if he could produce two novels like *Castle Richmond* and *Framley Parsonage* for every one of theirs he would not be far behind at the end of the day.'

2 SUMMARIES
AND
CRITICAL COMMENTARY

Chapter 1: who will be the new bishop?

Summary
The Bishop of Barchester, old Dr Grantly, is on the point of death and coincidentally the government is about to fall. It is generally felt in the town of Barchester that the bishop's son, Dr Grantly, who is archdeacon, will succeed him. Though new bishops are nominally appointed by the sovereign, in practice it is the Prime Minister who makes the appointment, and a new government is expected to favour the low church party in the Church of England rather than the high church, of which the archdeacon is a representative. The archdeacon cannot help wishing that his father will die before the government falls, since this is likely to be his last chance of a bishopric, but he falls on his knees and prays to be forgiven for such a desire. His father-in-law, Mr Harding, enters and finds him in this position. Shortly afterwards the bishop dies, having blessed both his son and Harding. The archdeacon's ambition is revived and he urges Harding to send a telegram at once to the Prime Minister, but Harding informs him that the government has already fallen. The telegram is sent, however, and forwarded to the new Prime Minister. The *Jupiter* (Trollope's name for *The Times*) announces that Dr Proudie, associated with the low church party, will be the new bishop, and the archdeacon's ambition is frustrated.

Commentary
This is one of the most striking opening chapters of any Victorian novel. The archdeacon is suddenly placed in a position in which his self-interest would seem to be dependent on his father dying as soon as possible. In a man of ambition who is also a Christian clergyman this is a particularly difficult conflict. Temptation is a common theme in a great many novels and the reader's conventional expectation is that those characters who resist it are good and those who succumb to

it are bad. The archdeacon's desire for his father's death, only stifled with difficulty, and then his eager attempt to serve his ambition after the death takes place encourage the reader to criticise the archdeacon and thus to feel morally superior to him, especially as the archdeacon professes to be a Christian but is driven by desires which the Christian is taught to despise. But it is characteristic of Trollope's fiction that it tends to undermine the assumptions or prejudices which govern such conventional judgements. After stressing that many will judge the archdeacon to be 'wicked', the narrator punctures this view-point – 'with such censures I cannot profess that I completely agree' – and proceeds to argue that the archdeacon's desires are part of human nature. To expect clergymen to be beyond such desires and thus to judge them by an unrealistic standard will only bring the clergy into disrepute. Thus the easy judgement of the archdeacon as a hypocrite is undercut. The novel suggests that the world cannot be made to conform to rigid moral categories since the archdeacon's ambition and his love for his father are both realities, even if they are not easily reconcilable in this situation. The failure of the archdeacon to achieve his ambition, however, is the first of many frustrations he has to suffer and suggests that those who are motivated by strong ambition in this novel are unlikely to be successful. The fact that this failure results from unfortunate chance is also interesting. The lives of several characters in the novel are significantly affected by chance, which suggests that Trollope shared the view of George Eliot in *The Mill on the Floss* that the Romantic idea that 'Character is Fate' must be qualified by taking circumstances into account. A person's life can be drastically altered by chance happenings, which in themselves may be quite trivial.

Chapter 2: Hiram's hospital according to act of parliament

Summary
This chapter recapitulates events in *The Warden*. Harding was warden of Hiram's charity hospital in Barchester, for which he received eight hundred pounds a year. A local reformer, John Bold, argued that the funds of the charity were being misused and he was supported by the *Jupiter*. Harding eventually resigned as warden but continued as rector of a small church, St. Cuthbert's, and as precentor (i.e. in charge of the singing of the choir) in the cathedral. Bold married Harding's daughter, Eleanor, after regretting his action. No new warden has yet been appointed and parliament has instituted reforms at the hospital. The new bishop will put these reforms into effect and appoint a new warden. John Bold has died, leaving Eleanor with a son and a substantial inheritance.

Commentary
Though this chapter is mainly concerned with background information, it possesses some interesting features. John Bold, who was perfectly healthy in *The Warden*, has since died, thus giving Trollope scope for an important element in the plot, namely competition for the hand of a rich widow. The narrator also distances himself by his tone from conventional responses. He does not feel much grief over the death of Bold, so that his 'Poor Eleanor', who looks very good in her widow's cap, has a slightly ironic ring. He also punctures conventional attitudes by pointing out how intolerable life would be if grief endured and describes the merits of Eleanor's baby in a somewhat satirical tone. Thus the narrator is established as a presence who comes between the reader and the material of the novel. It is clear that he views his characters and their concerns with an ironical detachment which is nevertheless sympathetic and which is seldom cynical. That is perhaps a difference between the narrator in Trollope and in Thackeray, the novelist he most admired.

Chapter 3: Dr and Mrs Proudie

Summary
Dr Proudie is established as bishop. He is a liberal in church matters, which causes him to be seen as useful by Whig politicians. He has also had much experience of serving on committees, though without having any power. He intends to spend as much time as he can in London, but since he does not possess substantial means, living economically in Barchester part of the year will suit him well. He is dominated by his wife, Mrs Proudie, in both domestic and religious matters. She is a strict believer in proper observance of the Sabbath and has promoted the career of Mr Obadiah Slope, the bishop's chaplain.

Commentary
The narrator explains the reasons for Dr Proudie's appointment as bishop. They have little to do with any positive merits he might possess. The political climate is such that a man of his type without very strong views on anything and who is prepared to adapt himself to virtually any situation is useful to politicians despite his lack of intellectual powers or business capacity. Thus the idea that men are appointed to bishoprics and other such posts on the basis of their merits or characters is undercut. The chapter also shows that judgements need to take account of all the facts. Though the new bishop is likely to be less popular than the previous bishop because he intends to live mainly in London and will thus not spend much money in Barchester, it must be understood that he is not a wealthy man like his predecessor and has many more commitments. Popularity in

Barchester depends considerably on what serves the self-interest of tradesmen. Even men who are successes in the eyes of the world also have their problems, and the bishop's main trial is his dominating wife. The narrator, however, undermines simple condemnation of Mrs Proudie as a shrew by pointing out that her religious views are sincerely held. Indeed, it is this combination of the desire to impose her will and sincere conviction that makes her such a formidable force.

Chapter 4: The bishop's chaplain

Summary
Mr. Slope's history and character are discussed. He made the acquaintance of Mrs Proudie in London where he was a young preacher. Since she was sympathetic to his theology she encouraged him and furthered his career through her influence with her husband. With an eye to a financially advantageous marriage he paid court to the Proudie's eldest daughter, Olivia, but withdrew on learning of the family's lack of wealth. His interest in Olivia revived when Dr Proudie was made bishop, but she rejected him. Slope is not discouraged and believes the bishop's lack of interest in the details of administration will allow him, effectively, to be bishop of Barchester. He knows that Mrs Proudie desires the same thing, but he believes he can outmanoeuvre her. Among his main assets are his power as a preacher and his popularity with women. He is strongly in sympathy with the low church and finds high church rituals offensive. Like Mrs Proudie, he is a strong sabbatarian. He is bound to arouse the opposition of the Barchester churchmen.

Commentary
At the beginning of the chapter we see an example of Trollope's literary playfulness when he informs the reader of the rumour that Slope is descended from the doctor 'who assisted at the birth of Mr T. Shandy', who exists only as a character in a work which mocks the conventions of the novel, Sterne's *Tristam Shandy*. Slope is the most ambitious character in the novel, a Tartuffe-like schemer who is determined to rise to power. Such a character usually plays the role of the villain, but Trollope departs from this literary stereotype in several ways. Slope is, despite his devious aims, a man who has 'both courage and spirit to bear him out in his resolution'. Though he is scheming to take over the bishop's functions, he is clearly a much more intelligent and capable and even religious man than the bishop. He also possesses genuine qualities, such as his power as a preacher. He is not simply a hypocrite, though he aims to use the church to serve his ambition. He is genuinely on the side of the low church, and

his contempt for the high church is based on principle and not mere strategy. The chapter contains a number of telling details about Slope's manner and appearance which flesh out the character and give him greater reality, such as his clammy handshake and his reddish face which resembles beef, 'beef, however, one would say, of a bad quality'. The information we are given about his scheming in the past, his wooing of Olivia, for example, suggests that he is liable to make miscalculations. This will be significant later. The novel continually views actions or decisions which on the surface appear to embody high principles in a somewhat ironic light. High principle is almost always inextricably mixed with self-interest or selfish motives. Thus the rejection by Olivia, a 'girl of spirit' with 'the blood of two peers in her veins', of Slope's renewed suit is slightly undercut when we are informed that she had 'another lover on the books', implying that her attitude might have been different if this had not been the case.

Chapter 5: A morning visit

Summary
The general belief in Barchester is that Mr Harding will be reinstated as warden of Hiram's hospital. On the second day after the bishop's arrival he and the archdeacon call at the bishop's palace. They are disconcerted at having to confront Mrs Proudie and Slope as well as the bishop. They are lectured on the evils of Sunday train journeys and the necessity for sabbath schools in Barchester. The archdeacon's attempt to change the subject to the comfort of the Proudies at the palace leads to a series of complaints about the palace's condition from the Proudies and Slope. After they make their escape, the archdeacon is ready to explode with anger and even the mild-tempered Harding almost loses his courteous manner.

Commentary
The plots of most novels are based to a greater or lesser degree on suspense. The first chapter had asked the question, 'Who will be the new bishop?', but the suspense was short-lived since we found out at the end of the chapter. In this novel, when one suspenseful situation is resolved, another tends to be created, somewhat playfully since Trollope does not have a high regard for suspense as a fictional device, as he makes clear in Chapter 15. The beginning of what is probably the most important suspense element of the plot took place in the previous chapter: namely, who will effectively be bishop? Since the bishop is a weak man, stronger characters will seek to exert power over him: his wife, Slope, the archdeacon. Who will triumph? Will the bishop outmanoeuvre them? In this chapter a different, though related suspense element emerges: who will be appointed to the

vacant wardenship? Those characters who seek to exercise power over the bishop have views on this matter and to succeed in persuading the bishop to act in accordance with these views will be an important factor in the struggle for power over the bishop. The visit of the archdeacon and Harding to the palace creates a situation that brings out the various attributes and traits of the characters involved. Dramatic tension is created by the power struggle that goes on between the archdeacon and the combination of Mrs Proudie and Slope, and the fact that the conventions of civility must be preserved. The archdeacon, who, when his father had been alive, had been the dominant figure in Barchester, now finds himself in danger of being dominated by these new forces who have entered his world of Barchester.

Chapter 6: War

Summary
The archdeacon is in a fury, is contemptuous of the bishop, but sees Slope as the real enemy, though Harding finds Mrs Proudie even more unsympathetic. The archdeacon's high church commitment, only moderate previously, is accentuated as a result of meeting Slope. He plans to encourage high church practices in order to frustrate Slope, though the idea of having to treat Slope as an equal in combat repels him. Slope is well aware that the archdeacon is his enemy and coolly works out his strategy. He contrives to preach in the cathedral the following Sunday and uses the occasion to mount an attack on high church practices which shocks the assembled Barchester clergy. He particularly attacks the intoning of the church service. This strikes at Harding. The bishop is surprised and shaken by the sermon.

Commentary
The title of this chapter, 'War', brings to the fore an important aspect of the novel: its comparison of the conflict between the high and low church parties to the kind of conflicts found in epic poetry. The previous chapter had described the archdeacon in an epic style of language: 'And now had I the pen of a mighty poet, would I sing in epic verse the noble wrath of the archdeacon.' This kind of language is used ironically to create a mock-heroic effect, the low and high church being seen in the context of the epic conflicts of such works as Homer's *The Iliad* or Milton's *Paradise Lost*. For the archdeacon, Slope is a kind of Satan who must be expelled from the paradise of Barchester. The mock-heroic tone should not disguise, however, that the Proudie and the Grantly parties represent an important nineteenth-century conflict. Slope's sermon brings this out when he attacks the formalism and ceremony of the high Anglican church. This is implicitly to attack the traditional social structure as being

outmoded and needing to be replaced by middle-class values. Tradition and the past should lose their dominant position in determining how society and its institutions are structured. The new realities of the present should have priority. But though this is a political and ideological conflict, the ideas underlying it are not given great emphasis in this novel, perhaps because they have been explored in the previous novel in the Barsetshire series, *The Warden*. The focus in *Barchester Towers* is on the people who identify with a particular position and how they seek to triumph over their opponents.

Chapter 7: The dean and chapter take counsel

Summary
The archdeacon is outraged by the sermon, but self-doubt is created in Harding, and he also wonders if the post of precentor is going to be taken away from him. Though the cathedral churchmen, known as the chapter, are incensed by the sermon, some of the poorer clergy, including the rector of Puddingdale, Mr Quiverful, aware of the power that Slope may exert in the diocese, react more favourably. The novelty of Slope's ideas also appeals to some of the congregation, especially women, who see him as representing progress. The archdeacon and other clergy, however, are determined to deny Slope any further opportunity to preach in the cathedral. This anti-Slope policy creates a pro-Slope party of women eager to listen to him outside the cathedral. The controversy encourages the Proudies to return to London, while Slope remains and seeks to increase his support.

Commentary
This chapter shows that no single view can be taken of Slope's sermon. Reactions to it are determined by a number of interests. Those of high church views are naturally outraged, but someone like Harding, with a tendency to self-doubt and introspection, worries that Slope may be right. Others without strong theological conviction are glad to hear something new that disturbs the normal dull routine, while clergymen whose well-being may depend on the support of Slope must take this into account in their response. Thus the novel shows the mixture of motives that shapes people's attitudes and responses in such a controversy. It would be superficial also to see it only as a religious conflict, for the division that it creates is more fundamentally political. The real threat posed by Slope's ideas is to the power exercised by the high church. We see the Grantly party taking political action against Slope by ensuring that he is denied further opportunity to preach in the cathedral.

Chapter 8: The ex-warden rejoices in his probable return to the hospital

Summary
Slope pays a visit to Eleanor Bold and her sister-in-law, Mary Bold. Clever flattery and praise of Harding overcomes their opposition on account of the sermon. Harding is displeased to hear of the visit, though he does not voice his displeasure. He is happy to announce that he is almost certain to be re-appointed warden, though on a reduced income and with twelve old women as well as twelve old men to look after. He is determined, however, not to make any request to Slope for favour. Eleanor attempts to defend Slope, and she and her father differ on the subject. She argues that Slope is justified on the grounds that he was expressing his sincere belief, but Harding replies that the discourtesy Slope showed in his sermon is indefensible.

Commentary
This chapter establishes the basis of another important element in the plot: Harding's and later the archdeacon's doubts over Eleanor's feelings towards Slope. This will lead to numerous misinterpretations and misjudgements later in the novel. In this chapter we see also Slope's cleverness in manipulating by flattery the women who are his main supporters. The narrator refers to the 'wiles of the serpent' to describe such cleverness, which calls to mind Satan's flattery of Eve in *Paradise Lost*. This echo fits in with the mock-epic aspect of the novel. Harding's difference of opinion with Eleanor over Slope's sermon establishes the humaneness and tolerance of his religious attitudes. The novel, however, suggests that a person's ideas cannot be dissociated from his or her nature. Harding expresses these views as if they are universally true, but they are clearly the product of his nature, just as the opposed views of Slope and the archdeacon are the product of their natures.

Chapter 9: The Stanhope family

Summary
Dr Vesey Stanhope, an absentee clergyman, has lived in Italy for twelve years, having gone there initially to seek a cure for a sore throat Slope writes to him as part of a campaign against such abuses in the church and threatens him with an investigation. Dr Stanhope and family return to Barchester and we are introduced to them individually. Dr Stanhope has little interest in religious matters. His wife only cares about her clothes. His elder daughter, Charlotte, runs the household. His younger daughter, the beautiful Madeline, had married an Italian, Paolo Neroni, a captain in the Pope's guard. The marriage was a disaster and she returned to live with the family,

crippled and with a baby daughter. Her explanation was that her condition was the result of a fall, but rumour has it that her husband was responsible. Since she can walk only in an ugly fashion, which would undermine her attraction to men, she lies on and is carried about on a sofa. The son of the family, Ethelbert (Bertie), is a dilettante who has never settled on a career or a religion. He was even for a time a Jew. Both the Proudie and the Grantly parties hope to recruit the Stanhopes to their cause.

Commentary
As the Grantly party represents the high church and the Proudie party the low church, the Stanhopes represent another aspect of the Church of England: the scope it offers to those who have no strong belief or particular interest in religion. Both the high church and the low church parties might be expected under normal circumstances to disapprove of such people, but in the Barchester situation of conflict between high and low church, each sees the Stanhopes as possible allies in the struggle against the other. Thus we see how politics influence viewpoint. The Stanhopes are particularly important to the novel as a whole since they bring an element of danger into the secure and insulated world of Barchester, particularly Madeline and Bertie. Both are prepared to criticise destructively, Bertie with a charming naivety and Madeline out of more sadistic motives. In the world of Barchester Bertie's irresponsible, carefree attitude and Madeline's siren-like sexual attractiveness are also potentially threatening. Charlotte Stanhope is a less important character but she is subtly characterised. Without her efforts the family would have disintegrated, but in order to establish her own position of power in the family she has encouraged the various vices of the others so that they are unable to reform and alter their situation. Thus what on the surface appear to be admirable qualities – energy, leadership – are open to a very different interpretation. One can also see a parallel between her and Mrs Proudie. In both the Proudie and the Stanhope families, male inadequacy – weakness and laziness respectively – has allowed a dominant woman to gain effective power. The novel suggests that in such situations power will tend to be exercised irresponsibly. The explicitness of Madeline's sexuality is unusual in a Victorian novel. The reason for her marriage to Neroni was almost certainly pregnancy, since we are told 'she had probably no alternative' and returned to her father's house six months later with a baby. Such experience has taught her that sex allows a woman to exercise power over men as long as the woman remains in control of the situation. In Barchester she will certainly not meet men like Neroni who could prove to be a threat.

Chapter 10: Mrs Proudie's reception – commenced

Summary
After Slope's sermon, the bishop is undecided about what to do, but Mrs Proudie's wholehearted approval of it makes him reluctant to criticise Slope. He thinks it politic, therefore, to leave Barchester and claims that government business demands it. Slope remains and pursues plans for Sabbath schools and the stopping of Sunday trains. On their return after two months, the Proudies hold a large evening party. The archdeacon decides that respect for the office of bishop demands that he attend. The Stanhopes are also invited, though Dr Stanhope disapproves of Madeline attending because he fears her habit of flirtation will be shocking. She has contacted Slope in advance and arranged for a sofa to be available for her. She makes a spectacular entrance.

Commentary
An important detail occurs in this chapter when Dr Stanhope meets Slope and the narrator comments: 'The doctor, in spite of his long absence, knew an English gentleman when he saw him', indicating that Slope is not one. The concept of the gentleman is an important one in the Victorian period, and it was particularly influential on Trollope. It is probably the main reason why the novel takes a negative view of Slope. His calculation, his self-interested manoeuvrings, his lack of principle are not criticised in an abstract moral context but are seen in relation to his not being a gentleman. For further discussion of this point see 'Characterisation' in Section 4.2 below. This chapter reveals again that people have mixed motives for their actions and decisions, as we see in the various reasons why people choose to attend the party. The Grantlyites attend for reasons of policy; Eleanor and Mary Bold because everyone else will be there; Mrs Stanhope to show her family off to Barchester society; Madeline to create a sensation and to arouse the jealousy of parsons' wives by having parsons at her feet. Madeline also ensures that she does create a sensational entrance not merely by the manner of her arrival but by arriving late and thus arousing interest as to who is to occupy the sofa. Her strong-mindedness is evident in her total lack of self-pity concerning her disability and the way she manipulates it for her own ends. The manner in which both she and Bertie are dressed for the party creates a comic effect and also shows how much they are outsiders in the world of Barchester.

Chapter 11: Mrs Proudie's reception – concluded

Summary
The bishop is confused because he does not know who Madeline and Bertie are. Since the bishop and Bertie are trapped behind the sofa, Bertie moves it and it rolls onto Mrs Proudie's dress, tearing it. The tone of Bertie's apologies and Madeline's laughter enrage Mrs Proudie, and she retreats angrily to change. Madeline charms the bishop, but he is annoyed when he finally finds out who she is. Bertie disconcerts the assembled clergy with his religious history and his praise for German professors. The bishop takes Harding aside, offers him the wardenship, and invites him to discuss with Slope the changes that will take place. Slope meanwhile has fallen under the spell of Madeline despite Mrs Proudie's disapproval and her efforts to separate him and Madeline. After the party is over, with Madeline last to go, Mrs Proudie is left 'by no means contented with the result of her first grand party at Barchester'.

Commentary
This is the most comic chapter in the novel, the comedy mainly deriving from the confrontation between the Stanhopes and the Proudies. The two most striking moments are the slapstick of the moving sofa and Bertie's theological discussion with the bishop, culminating in his remark, 'I was a Jew once myself'. More than comedy is at work in the chapter, though, for here we see the subversive force of the Stanhopes. Mrs Proudie can dominate almost everybody but she cannot intimidate Madeline or Bertie, and the damage Madeline's sofa inflicts on Mrs Proudie's dress is emblematic of Madeline's victory in their first encounter. The narrator again uses epic language for comic effect, as in the following epic or Homeric simile: 'As Juno may have looked at Paris on Mount Ida so did Mrs Proudie look on Ethelbert Stanhope when he pushed the leg of the sofa into her lace train.' Bertie's inability to treat such men as the bishop and the archdeacon with deference allows him to point out to them some uncomfortable facts, for example that English universities could learn much from their German counterparts. Another important element of the chapter is that it shows the roots of Slope's ultimate fall. We see that his attraction towards Madeline is not reconcilable with retaining the favour of Mrs Proudie.

Chapter 12: Slope versus Harding

Summary
Harding receives a rather impolite note from Slope asking him to come to the palace at nine thirty next morning. Slope keeps him waiting for half an hour and then warns him that the wardenship will

now have a reduced salary and more duties than previously. He tries to annoy Harding by criticising the former arrangements and by implication the late bishop. He particularly hurts Harding by asserting that new men are 'carting away the useless rubbish of past centuries'. Harding disconcerts Slope by asking what the situation will be if he accepts the appointment but refuses to perform such tasks as supervising a Sabbath-day school for Barchester's poor children, since he does not think such duties can be imposed on whoever is appointed. Slope obstructs Harding's desire to see the bishop personally to discuss the matter and tries to make Harding either accept or reject the post. But Harding replies that he will not accept if it is conditional on performing the new duties. Slope chooses to take this as rejection and reports back to the bishop. The bishop is disappointed, but Mrs Proudie is pleased and puts forward Mr Quiverful as a better candidate. The bishop agrees that Slope should see Quiverful.

Commentary
Here we see Slope's cleverness at manipulating situations and people so as to place himself in a position of power. He keeps Harding waiting and criticises the late bishop in order to put Harding into a frame of mind in which he might act rashly. This is a situation in which Harding's lack of assertiveness is something of an advantage. It allows him to come off better than he might have done if he had a stronger sense of his own dignity and self-esteem. Though hurt by Slope's implication that he is a useless relic of the past, he does not allow his emotions to get the better of him and he troubles Slope with his question, 'But if I accept the appointment, and yet disagree with the bishop, what then?' Slope had not anticipated this turn of events and has no answer. He does not succeed in his plan to make Harding withdraw, and he is forced to resort to lying to the bishop and Mrs Proudie in claiming that Harding had absolutely refused the appointment. Slope's trump card in this confrontation is that he is in a position to deny Harding access to the bishop and can then choose to present the bishop with his own interpretation of what took place. It is this role as the bishop's intermediary that gives Slope the opportunity to exercise power. As we shall see later, only very determined action can overcome such power. There is some dramatic irony in the chapter, for Slope's effort to deprive Harding of the wardenship rebounds on him when he later decides that it is in his interest to support him. This then becomes another source of division between him and Mrs Proudie.

Chapter 13: The rubbish cart

Summary
Harding is depressed at the outcome of his meeting with Slope,

especially by the thought that he is a useless relic of the past. On his way to see the archdeacon about the matter he calls in on Eleanor and is surprised to learn that Slope had discussed the wardenship with her the day before. Slope's presentation of the situation to Eleanor had been very different from the way he had presented it to Harding, since he had given her the impression that everything possible was being done to re-appoint Harding. Eleanor had agreed to help with the new Sabbath school. Harding warns her against Slope but she denies that she has any intention of being guided by the chaplain. Nevertheless, Harding thinks she may have sided with Slope. In the afternoon he talks with his other daughter, Susan Grantly, the wife of the archdeacon, at Plumstead. She is strongly on the side of the Grantly party and is shocked that Eleanor should be receiving visits from Slope. She thinks it likely that Slope's aim is to marry Eleanor for her money and believes that he may succeed, which makes Harding even more depressed. The narrator informs us, however, that Slope is ignorant of Eleanor's fortune and that she has no thought of remarrying.

Commentary
Though we have seen that Harding's lack of a sense of his own dignity was an advantage in his confrontation with Slope, when he is on his own it leads to inwardness and self-conscious reflection that make it difficult for him to think positively or act decisively. He is inclined to think that Slope may be right to see him as 'useless rubbish'. This frame of mind does not help him to understand Eleanor's relation to Slope, especially as Slope's strategy of playing different roles with different people has given her the opposite impression of him from that formed by her father. We also see how misinterpretations can be created by fear and prejudice in Susan Grantly's deduction on the basis of very little evidence that Slope and Eleanor are likely to marry. This possibility places Harding in something of a dilemma, since he has ample reason to distrust Slope yet he is morally committed to the view that one must allow others to make their own decisions and not try to impose one's own judgement on them. The narrator's assurance that these fears of Eleanor marrying Slope are groundless is one of many examples in the novel of a refusal to exploit a sense of suspense.

Chapter 14: The new champion

Summary
The archdeacon returns from Oxford for dinner. He announces triumphantly that the Reverend Francis Arabin is to become vicar of St Ewold's, a parish on the outskirts of Barchester which is in the gift of the archdeacon. Arabin, a fellow of Lazarus College, Oxford, is a

respected and scholarly high churchman who has engaged in controversy with Slope. Arabin is 'so high' a churchman that he almost
succumbed to the temptation of the 'cesspool of Rome'. The archdeacon and Dr Gwynne, the Master of Lazarus College, persuade
him that it is his duty to help to defeat Slope. When Harding tells of
his experience at the palace, the archdeacon asserts that the bishop
has no right to make changes at Hiram's hospital and resolves to call
on the bishop himself, though Harding is worried that a new
controversy will spring up over the wardenship. In their bedroom,
Mrs Grantly tells her husband of her fears of a marriage between
Eleanor and Slope, and he immediately believes the worst. Next
morning this makes the archdeacon less than cordial to Harding.

Commentary
As Slope is seen by the archdeacon as the bishop's champion, the
archdeacon therefore seeks out a champion for himself in this epic
conflict. Arabin and Slope are thus parallel characters. Both are
clergymen, both are outsiders to Barchester, and both will be
attracted to the same two women, Eleanor and Madeline. A significant difference between them, however, is that, as the archdeacon
states, Arabin is 'a gentleman in every respect'. The novel is more
interested in the temperamental conflict between the two characters
than the theological one, which is not discussed in much detail.
Indeed, Slope's and Arabin's previous encounter over the subject of
the apostolic succession was a 'war' which was carried on 'merrily' in
the pages of the *Jupiter*, suggesting that the issue was a mere pretext
for point scoring. The archdeacon's readiness to believe that Eleanor
is likely to marry Slope is another example of how fear and prejudice
can determine one's viewpoint and lead to premature conclusions
being drawn.

Chapter 15: The widow's suitors

Summary
Slope visits Mr Quiverful at Puddingdale to offer him the wardenship. Quiverful, with a wife and fourteen children to support on only
four hundred pounds a year, is grateful but is worried that he may
offend Harding. He remarks casually that Eleanor is rich, having
twelve hundred pounds a year, and that Harding probably plans to
live with her. Slope's interest in Eleanor increases immediately, but
switching his allegiance back to Harding will be difficult because of
Mrs Proudie's view of the situation. Another complicating factor is
that Slope is also attracted by Madeline and does not want to give up
visiting her. He is not prepared, however, to withdraw his opposition
to the archdeacon to further his chances with Eleanor. The Stanhopes
have also found out about Eleanor's fortune, and Charlotte suggests

that if Bertie married her this would solve his problems. Bertie agrees to this plan somewhat half-heartedly. Madeline is informed. She is cynical about marriage and dismisses Eleanor as 'vapid' and ill-dressed. The narrator reassures the reader that neither Slope nor Bertie will marry Eleanor.

Commentary

This chapter is notable for its undermining of conventional narrative expectations. Both Slope's and Charlotte Stanhope's awareness of Eleanor's fortune and how attractive this makes her as a marriage partner conforms to a plot structure that any experienced novel reader will be familiar with. 'Who will marry the heroine?' is a standard feature of the plots of thousands of novels. Also, marrying for money is what one usually expects of the villain. Such elements are traditionally used to create suspense for the reader: who will the heroine marry, will she succumb to the villain, etc? It is in this chapter that Trollope most drastically undermines suspense by informing the reader that Eleanor will marry neither Slope nor Bertie, even if whom she will marry is not disclosed. The narrator goes on to express his disapproval of suspense as a narrative device – 'Our doctrine is, that the author and the reader should move along together in full confidence with each other' – but this doctrine is only partially put into effect, even though the reader may have a good idea whom Eleanor will finally marry. The novel also exploits the undermining of suspense to achieve certain artistic effects. For example, it functions as a playful undercutting of normal narrative expectations and thus acts as a kind of alienation effect, that is, interrupting the reader's identification with the fiction and thus encouraging greater awareness and self-consciousness in the act of reading. One is made aware of how easily the narrator of a novel can manipulate the reader. In freeing the reader from concern as to whether or not Slope or Bertie will marry Eleanor, the reader can see this part of the plot more disinterestedly and thus appreciate to a greater extent the comedy of the situation. We can concentrate more on character than on how the plot will turn out. For further discussion of this aspect of the novel see Chapter 4 below on 'Technical features'.

Though it is conventional for the villain of a novel to inveigle an heiress or a rich woman into marriage, Slope's motives are not totally selfish. Money, he thinks, would help to promote the interests of his religion. Slope is not a simple villain with blatantly selfish motives. His self-esteem is dependent on his seeing his motives as not governed by purely selfish considerations, and though the narrator implies that this is a rationalisation, any expectation that the reader has that Slope is the conventional villain who is consciously self-seeking and cynically hypocritical is undercut. In this chapter we also see Madeline as a negative force who punctures accepted ideas with wit and contempt. This is revealed in her attack on marriage as 'tyranny on one side, and deceit on the the other'. Her views are allowed to stand on their own and are not placed in the narrative in such a way that we are encouraged to discount them. This is unusual in the context of the Victorian novel.

Chapter 16: Baby worship

Summary
Slope calls on Eleanor while she and Mary Bold are playing with the baby. The narrator compares the beauty of Eleanor and Madeline. Slope has had confirmation of Eleanor's fortune and has spoken to the bishop in favour of Harding. But the bishop is reluctant to disobey his wife's wishes, especially as she has been in touch with Mrs Quiverful. Slope tries artfully to create desire for rebellion on the bishop's part. The bishop still believes Harding is entitled to the wardenship but he does not know what to do. The fact that Slope and his wife are divided is, however, a pleasant surprise. Slope endeavours to ingratiate himself with Eleanor. He pretends that he thought Harding did not want the wardenship. She assures him that he does but does not think that the post can now be denied to a man who has fourteen children. She also refuses to see the bishop herself. Though Slope claims to be committed to Harding, Eleanor is not wholly convinced of his good faith and is pessimistic about her father's chances of regaining the wardenship.

Commentary
The narrator gently satirises Eleanor's and Mary's baby worship, though it brings out the womanliness and femininity of Eleanor which make her attractive to men. The beauty of Eleanor and Madeline is compared in such a way as to make one sympathise with the fact that Slope and later Arabin are attracted to both. After Slope is announced, the narrator breaks off to consider what happened previously in Slope's meeting with the bishop. This shift from present to past happens repeatedly in the novel. Such a disruption of continuity of time can be seen as another form of alienation effect. Though conventional novel readers, whose main interest is in following the story, may find this irritating, it does ultimately work for the benefit of the reader, since one can read the interview between Eleanor and Slope in a much fuller context. Slope's decision to seek to marry Eleanor is a crucial one since it makes it inevitable that he will come into conflict with Mrs Proudie. He decides that he must now support Harding for the wardenship, but he does not realise that Mrs Proudie has already informed Mrs Quiverful that her husband will gain the post. When Slope hears of this he takes the fateful decision to oppose Mrs Proudie and adopts the strategy of encouraging the bishop to

rebel. The bishop in turn thinks he can exploit the division between his wife and Slope to his own advantage by using Slope to help gain the ascendancy over his wife. Supporting Harding for warden is necessary for Slope's marriage plans since it gives him the opportunity both to gain Eleanor's gratitude and to manoeuvre her into forming an alliance with him in the effort to overcome the difficulties in the way of Harding's becoming warden. Though Eleanor intends to keep her distance, Slope cleverly manipulates the situation so that they are drawn more closely together, symbolised by his gradually moving his chair closer to hers as their conversation goes on.

Chapter 17: Who shall be cock of the walk?

Summary
Since he can count on Slope's support against his wife, the bishop believes he has the opportunity to escape her power. The archdeacon has requested an appointment, which the bishop suspects will be about the wardenship. Since he will have to give the archdeacon an answer, he decides to confront his wife. Finding her with their three daughters, he cannot sustain his determination and discloses that Slope now believes that Harding should be warden. The bishop tells Slope that Mrs Proudie's will in the matter is to be obeyed. Later Slope is visited by Mrs Proudie. She criticises his behaviour with Madeline at the party and his visiting her subsequently. Slope controls himself and merely points out that he has no interest in Madeline. She also accuses him of interfering too much in the bishop's business. Slope realises that his anticipated struggle for power against Mrs Proudie has now begun in earnest.

Commentary
Conflict between two powerful forces can provide an opportunity for the weak, and the bishop hopes to exploit this situation and escape from his wife's tyranny. Trollope employs the language of war for mock-epic comic effect in characterising the bishop's efforts to get himself into a strong frame of mind for the conflict, only to create anti-climax when the bishop's resolve disintegrates: 'Return, bishop, to thy sanctum on the lower floor, and postpone thy combative propensities for some occasion in which at least thou mayest fight the battle against odds less tremendously against thee.' The bishop's failure only alerts Mrs Proudie to Slope's actions and brings the conflict between her and Slope to a head. Mrs Proudie's instinct is to take the offensive when challenged. Her power lies in her complete certainty that she is in the right. Slope is capable of engaging in direct combat when the occasion demands it, but he can also exercise restraint when necessary, as he does when Mrs Proudie confronts him. It is clear they will be well matched in the conflict to follow.

Chapter 18: The widow's persecution

Summary
The next day the bishop finds that his health will not permit him to see the archdeacon and delegates this task to Slope. By the bishop's indicating to Slope that Mrs Proudie is listening outside the door, Slope realises that the bishop is on his side and that the appointment of Quiverful as warden is to be his last submission to his wife's power. The archdeacon refuses to see Slope and seeks out Harding at Eleanor's house. Her view that he should have seen Slope arouses his indignation. She does not know that he thinks she might be contemplating marriage to Slope. Despite his dislike of Slope, Harding is prepared to accept him as Eleanor's husband. The archdeacon's suspicions of a possible marriage are increased when he hears the reasons for Slope's last visit to Eleanor. Harding is willing to give up his claim to the wardenship but the archdeacon refuses to accept this. He writes to the bishop reasserting Harding's claim and invites Harding to Plumstead to discuss the matter with Arabin. Eleanor is also invited, with a view to keeping her away from Slope. She accepts but can only come a day later since she has arranged a visit to the Stanhopes. She assures the archdeacon, who suspects that Slope might be there, that the Stanhopes are not having a party and thus that she will be the only guest.

Commentary
One of the advantages of 'omniscient' narration, that is, the narrator's knowledge of the minds of all the characters, is that it allows the novelist to exploit misunderstandings between the characters and observe their misinterpretations of each other. In this novel, the effect is mainly comic. The archdeacon, suspecting that Eleanor is romantically involved with Slope, interprets her remark that he should have seen Slope in that context. Eleanor, unaware of the assumptions that are being made about her relationship with Slope, feels that she is being treated badly for no reason. Harding's determination to be fair-minded and unprejudiced with regard to Slope ironically only makes the situation worse since it prevents him saying anything to resolve matters. Trollope often uses the relation between narrator and reader to create an ironical interplay in the narrative. Thus the narrator judges Harding's desire to be unprejudiced as weakness on the grounds that the reader will naturally take the same view of Slope as the archdeacon, yet the archdeacon's opinion of Slope is largely made up of prejudice and misinterpretation.

Chapter 19: Barchester by moonlight

Summary
Next day at the Stanhopes Dr Stanhope receives a bill for seven hundred pounds which Bertie owes. He is annoyed by this, especially at Bertie's indifference on the subject, but Charlotte prevents matters coming to a head by hinting at the possibility of a marriage between Bertie and Eleanor. In the evening Eleanor arrives for her visit, but she is surprised when Slope also calls. He is uncomfortable at finding the woman he plans to marry and the woman he plans to enjoy a flirtation with in the same room. Eleanor is, however, unaware of Slope's discomfort since Bertie is devoting his attention to her. Charlotte arranges a walk in the moonlight for herself and Slope, and Bertie and Eleanor. They pass Hiram's hospital and Eleanor tells Bertie of recent developments concerning her father. Bertie advises her not to trust Slope. She is favourably impressed with the Stanhopes, particularly Bertie, as a result of her visit.

Commentary
As in his treatment of Slope, with the Stanhopes Trollope undermines the reader's tendency to resort to simple condemnation of such characters. Though heartless, lazy, irreligious and mercenary, their vices should not be seen in isolation but in relation to other qualities they possess that cannot be easily condemned. They bear any sufferings without self-pity. They are optimistic, but if such optimism fails, they are stoical. Madeline, though crippled, retains her strong-mindedness and courage and does not complain about her fate. Bertie's amorality goes together with a carefree attitude that is on the side of life. We also see in this chapter, in the treatment of Bertie's indebtedness to a Jew, that though Trollope exposes the prejudices of his characters and calls the reader's prejudices into question by undermining his or her conventional assumptions, he holds some prejudices of his own, as is shown in his presentation of the Jewish moneylender, which only reinforces a stereotype. The chapter also shows the problems that Slope's admiration for two women are going to create for him, and exploits the humour of the situation, referring to Eleanor, for example, as his 'embryo spouse'. Joseph Wiesenfarth has some interesting comments on this chapter in his essay on the novel; see 'Further Reading'.

Chapter 20: Mr Arabin

Summary
Arabin arrives at Plumstead on the day that Eleanor is visiting the Stanhopes. We learn more about him. He is forty and a bachelor. After resisting the attractions of Catholicism and deciding to stay in

the Church of England he had become a favourite of Dr Gwynne and a defender of high Anglicanism. Susan Grantly and her two daughters, however, are not impressed by him. Though he has a reputation for wit, he is not happy, since he has realised that he is strongly attracted to the good things of life but thinks that they have now passed him by; yet he has not risen in the church either.

Commentary
Barchester Towers was originally published in three volumes, and this is the first chapter of volume two. It is important to be aware of this, since volume one and volume two are in some ways parallel. For example, Arabin plays a role in volume two that is similar to Slope's role in volume one. Both come from outside the world of Barchester, are seen as the main defenders of the religious position they support, and are attracted by the same two women. Arabin is the kind of character, however, who tends to appear uninteresting or colourless in a novel, especially in comparison with a character such as Slope. He therefore presents certain artistic difficulties which we can see Trollope endeavouring to overcome. This may explain why Trollope goes into considerable detail about his religious background. This wider context gives added weight to the character. In an understated way it emerges that Arabin, like Slope, is an ambitious man, though he has accepted only reluctantly that he has worldly longings: 'He had professed himself indifferent to mitres and diaconal residences, to rich livings and pleasant glebes, and now he had to own to himself that he was sighing for the good things of other men, on whom, in his pride, he had ventured to look down.' But whereas Slope is always on the look-out for opportunities to serve his own interest, Arabin is inclined to be self-doubting and is unable to pursue his self-interest with Slope's single-mindedness.

Chapter 21: St Ewold's parsonage

Summary
When Harding and Eleanor arrive at Plumstead next day, the archdeacon and Arabin are out, having gone to see the church at St Ewold. Eleanor talks with her sister, who finds out that Slope was also at the Stanhopes. Eleanor defends him against Susan's criticism, which Susan interprets as a sign of romantic interest. Eleanor remains oblivious to this suspicion. When the archdeacon is told that Slope was at the Stanhopes, he believes that Eleanor has deliberately misled him. In contrast to her visit to the Stanhopes, Eleanor finds the evening very dull. Arabin displays little interest in her. Next day they all go to St Ewold's parsonage. Eleanor and Arabin draw closer together as a result of light-hearted banter about the need of a priest for a priestess. Alone with Arabin, Eleanor is impressed that he takes

his religion very seriously. They inspect the vicarage. The archdeacon criticises the size of the dining room but Arabin thinks that expensive structural alterations are not justifiable.

Commentary
Eleanor's presence at Plumstead gives further scope for misunderstanding and misinterpretation of her relationship with Slope. We see how preconceptions influence interpretation when the fact that Slope had been at the Stanhopes when Eleanor had previously said she was to be the only guest reinforces the Grantly view that she is romantically involved with Slope. Eleanor displays a certain naivety and lack of intelligence in failing to realise how her relationship with Slope is being interpreted. Since the reader is placed in a position of knowing how the characters misunderstand each other, this creates considerable scope for comedy. In Arabin's discussion of his religious position, we see that he is an extreme conservative who stops short, however, of the Church of Rome, clearly the unacceptable face of conservatism for Trollope. This chapter also shows how the structure of the novel works in terms of parallelism and contrast. Arabin's attitude in regard to his new residence is in marked contrast to the Proudies' and Slope's criticism of the bishop's palace in Chapter 5.

Chapter 22: The Thornes of Ullathorne

Summary
The following Sunday Arabin has to preach his first sermon in his new church. The archdeacon will assist him and Eleanor will accompany them. Between services they are to have lunch at the squire's house. Wilfred Thorne, the squire of Ullathorne, and his sister, Miss Monica Thorne, are both unmarried and extreme conservatives. They regard families dating back only to James I with contempt. Mr Thorne regarded the repeal of the corn laws as such a betrayal that he even stopped hunting rather than consort with those who supported repeal. His sister is even more extreme than he is and can find nothing good about the modern world. The live in Ullathorne Court, a Tudor manor house, which is described in considerable detail.

Commentary
The two new characters introduced in this chapter, Mr and Miss Thorne, have an important social role in the novel. They are representatives of the traditional squirearchy and of an outmoded form of conservatism which, nevertheless, is shown in an attractive light. The narrator's satirical tone, particularly in the case of Miss Thorne, is one of benign amusement at their excesses, Miss Thorne, for example, being a 'pure Druidess' in religion. In a novel not noted for detailed description, the long description of their house stands

out. This reinforces the Thornes' rootedness, a quality the narrator admires: 'May it be long before their number diminishes.' However, since both the Thornes are unmarried, they seem to be a dying breed. But though there is a strong element of affection in the presentation of these representatives of a rooted Englishness that may be passing, the narrator indicates that the Thornes' nostalgia for the past is based largely on ignorance, and he is clearly sceptical that there was ever any golden age in the past: 'She imagined that a purity had existed which was now gone; that a piety had adorned our pastors and simple docility our people, for which it may be feared history gave her but little true account.'

Chapter 23: Mr Arabin reads himself in a St Ewold's

Summary
Despite Arabin's nervousness he preaches well and makes a favourable impression on his congregation. At lunch with the Thornes, Miss Thorne gives Eleanor advice on her baby's teething; Mr Thorne has detailed conversations with the archdeacon and Arabin, discussing fertiliser with the one and church matters with the other. The archdeacon preaches in the afternoon, and after the service he, Arabin and Eleanor return to Plumstead.

Commentary
As Slope preached a sermon in the first volume of the novel, Arabin preaches a sermon here. But the parallelism only brings out the contrast in the approaches of both men to religious matters. Whereas Slope was confident and intent on creating conflict and antagonism, Arabin is lacking in confidence and shy at the prospect of encountering his congregation. Both Slope's and Arabin's texts are on the surface similar, since each is about the need to adhere to God's truth, but Arabin does not set out to annoy or antagonise but to reassure and unite his congregation and he succeeds in doing so. Arabin is thus well received at St Ewold's. He is a man who seeks to bring the community together, in contrast to Slope, who is determined to create conflict. We see how deep-rooted Miss Thorne's conservative views are, since even a subject such as a child's teething is a pretext for attacking the modern age. But the satire is gentle.

Chapter 24: Mr Slope manages matters very cleverly at Puddingdale

Summary
Two pleasant weeks are passed at Plumstead. At a dinner party at the Stanhopes, Mr Arabin's attention to Madeline displeases Eleanor, even though she is with Bertie and prefers him to Arabin. The

archdeacon is at a loss to how he can attain direct contact with the bishop. Arabin advises him to seek the help of Dr Gwynne, the master of Lazarus, since the bishop cannot refuse to see both of them. Having decided to support Harding for the wardenship even though it will create conflict with Mrs Proudie, Slope sees Quiverful at Puddingdale and points out that his appointment was dependent on Harding not wanting the post, but now it seems he wants it. Though disappointed, Quiverful feels he must withdraw. Mrs Quiverful's anticipation of disaster seems justified. Slope returns to Barchester in order to persuade the bishop to support Harding.

Commentary

Like Slope in volume one, Arabin succumbs to the charms of Madeline. At this stage Eleanor does not think she has any romantic feeling for Arabin, but her slight annoyance at his behaviour suggests an attraction she is not yet aware of, though she interprets her irritation with him as disappointment that he should be drawn to someone like Madeline. The characters not only tend to misinterpret others, they misinterpret themselves. Arabin likewise has no conscious awareness of any attraction towards Eleanor. The potential for love is there, though neither recognises it. Both the archdeacon and Slope are faced with difficulties. The archdeacon's forte is his energy and courage in situations of confrontation, but he can do little to oppose a bishop who will not enter into any direct contact. Though the bishop is a weak man with Slope and Mrs Proudie, with whom he cannot avoid contact, this weakness does not mean he is always powerless, as his negation of the power of the archdeacon shows. As the bishop exerts power over the archdeacon by refusing to enter into confrontation, Slope has decided that confrontation with Mrs Proudie is now unavoidable. Since the desire for power is the main driving force of his character, this contest cannot be avoided if he is to triumph. However, Slope has not only the power of Mrs Proudie to face; though he does not anticipate it, he will also be faced with the power of Mrs Quiverful's reaction to the withdrawal of the offer of the wardenship from her husband. Powerful women prove to be Slope's undoing throughout the novel, which is ironical since his rise has been the result of the influence he has been able to exert over women.

Chapter 25: Fourteen arguments in favour of Mr Quiverful's claims

Summary

Mrs Quiverful is incensed at Slope and resolves to see Mrs Proudie, without telling her husband. She persuades a neighbouring farmer to take her to Barchester and bribes her way into the palace. Mrs Proudie has just exerted her power once again over the bishop by making him refuse an invitation from the archbishop because it does not include her. When she hears Mrs Quiverful's story, her brow darkens and she goes off to see the bishop, asking Mrs Quiverful to wait. Mrs Quiverful reminds her that the future of fourteen children is at stake.

Commentary
Here we see the power of women in action. We have seen earlier that the main source of Slope's power lies in the fact that the bishop's fear of direct contact gives Slope the opportunity to operate as an intermediary and as a kind of double agent, manipulating both the bishop himself and those who seek contact with or are dependent on the bishop for his own purposes. He exercises this power with Quiverful, by claiming that it is the bishop's will that Harding be warden. Having forced Quiverful to withdraw he can then tell the bishop that Quiverful has withdrawn and that there is now no obstacle to the re-appointment of Harding as warden. Quiverful is powerless against Slope, but Slope does not take Mrs Quiverful into account. Her force of character has an almost elemental quality, since the well-being of her fourteen children is at stake. There seem to be insuperable obstacles in her way: the cleverness of Slope's procedure, the problem of getting to Barchester without a carriage since a long walk is out of the question for her, and then being admitted to the palace without an appointment; these obstacles are triumphantly overcome. Earlier Mrs Proudie also exemplified the power of women theme in compelling the bishop to turn down an invitation from the archbishop. But when Mrs Proudie finds out about Slope's actions, she knows that her power is being challenged.

Chapter 26: Mrs Proudie wrestles and gets a fall

Summary
Mrs Proudie finds Slope with the bishop. She demands to know by what authority he visited Quiverful. Slope proclaims his independence from her by stating that he is subject only to the bishop. She tries to make Slope leave the room so that she may speak to her husband alone, but Slope refuses to go. In asking the bishop whether Slope or herself should leave the room, the bishop replies that he and Slope are very busy. She leaves. Slope, triumphant, attempts to consolidate his advantage by pointing out the bishop's need to throw off his wife's yoke if he is not to be seen as contemptible. The bishop now accepts the archbishop's invitation, but he will not go so far as to write to Harding confirming his appointment as warden since he says he wants to see him first. Mrs Proudie goes to her bedroom defeated, but soon realises that she can reassert her dominance later when she and the bishop are alone. She then sees Mrs Quiverful, blames Mr

Quiverful for being weak in giving up his claim, but promises to do everything she can to help him be appointed.

Commentary
There has been a long build-up to this confrontation between Slope and Mrs Proudie; with such well-matched opponents the reader has the right to expect an exciting contest and is not disappointed. We see that sheer force of character and personality do not necessarily always win such struggles. Mrs Proudie's indignation against Slope and her husband makes her vulnerable in this situation to a more controlled opponent. Whereas she is full of rage, Slope is calculating. He is aware of the importance of the bishop in this confrontation while she assumes that the bishop is still totally in her power; hence her miscalculation, which allows Slope victory, even if only temporarily. It is also ironic that the power of Mrs Proudie should be defeated by such a mild remark as 'Why, my dear . . . Mr Slope and I are very busy.' What is powerful always depends on the context. Mrs Proudie gives her power away when she presents the bishop with the freedom to choose, and she has therefore no option but to accept his decision. Trollope shows his psychological penetration in his discussion of Slope's mistake in looking triumphantly at Mrs Proudie instead of more cleverly adopting a more placatory manner. Slope forgets that winning a battle does not necessarily mean winning the war. Also, being technically subject to the bishop he cannot hope to dominate him in the way that Mrs Proudie does, so that he fails crucially to make the victory one of real substance by not being able to persuade the bishop to make Harding's appointment a *fait accompli*. When those who live for power are defeated, the loss of self-esteem is particularly hard to bear, and Mrs Proudie's worst moment is when she has to tell Mrs Quiverful that she has failed. Only her realisation that she can fight another day, since the bishop cannot avoid seeing her alone in their bedroom, makes her able to cope with the situation. In accordance with the novel's continual undermining of the reader's conventional expectations, the narrator, in pointing out at the end of the chapter that Mrs Proudie was genuinely touched by Mrs Quiverful's situation, prevents her being seen merely as a virago intent on power.

Chapter 27: A love scene

Summary
Slope posts the bishop's letter to the archbishop, and writes to Eleanor telling her, in an over-familiar letter, that her father is assured of the wardenship. He leaves the letter at Eleanor's house. He cannot resist visiting Madeline. She feels certain that he has designs on Eleanor even though he has feelings of love for herself,

and she exploits this contradiction in his feelings. She forces him to admit that he loves her and then asks him directly if he is going to marry Eleanor, forcing him to lie. Madeline also exploits the contradictions between Slope's love for her and his Christian faith, since she makes him recognise that he would not be prepared to go so far as to marry her. Slope leaves her in a troubled state of mind.

Commentary
The narrator's advice to Slope that 'It's gude to be off with the auld luve / Before ye be on wi' the new' looks forward to Chapter 46, in which Madeline taunts Slope by quoting this maxim. However, Slope's courting of two women is not merely a sign of his lack of principle. Both women genuinely attract him, and though his interest would be served by devoting himself only to one, his head cannot rule his heart. It is ironic, therefore, that the calculating, self-seeking side of Slope is associated with the conventionally moral view that one should not court more than one woman at a time, and that the heart, which in most novels is identified with moral feeling, urges Slope in a conventionally immoral direction. In this chapter we see particularly clearly the darker side of Madeline's character. Slope's hypocrisy and self-seeking remain within the confines of the comic, But Madeline's sadistic side moves beyond that. The thought of corrupting a religious man has a genuine appeal to her mind, and this appeal is heightened since it would reinforce her belief that religion is simply a veneer with little power over the passions. However, there is no danger of Slope's passion for Madeline leading to an elopement, and this helps to keep their relationship within the realm of comedy. The narrator brings out the comedy in the following comment: 'It would be impossible to run away with a lady who required three servants to move her from a sofa.' Madeline, unlike Slope, does not seek to serve her purposes by disguising her true feelings or thoughts. She states the truth about herself when she declares that she has no heart and that it would be wiser of him to marry Eleanor. It is Slope who chooses to become entangled in her web. Slope does, however, have one opportunity to assert his power over her, when she urges him to run off with her. Madeline is playing a game with him, but if he had realised this and pretended to take her at her word she would have been placed in a difficult situation. But he does not call her bluff and thus allows her to triumph.

Chapter 28: Mrs Bold is entertained by Dr and Mrs Grantly at Plumstead

Summary
Harding and the archdeacon call at Eleanor's house in Barchester and they are given Slope's letter to deliver. The archdeacon is

indignant and believes Harding should open it and take any steps necessary to stop this romance. Harding, however, believes that Eleanor has the right to free choice. Eleanor is at first pleased at Slope's news regarding the wardenship but feels that the over-familiar tone is offensive. Dinner is difficult since Eleanor perceives that there has been talk about her receiving the letter. Arabin has been told of the archdeacon's fears. At the archdeacon's request, Mrs Grantly speaks to Eleanor after dinner, but Eleanor defends Slope since she does not realise that she is suspected of being romantically involved with him. Harding is shown the letter but does not react as Eleanor expects, as he is displeased both by its tone and by Slope's acting on his behalf. He feels that Slope must have been encouraged by Eleanor but does not speak about the matter and so clear up the misunderstanding. The archdeacon asks Eleanor to see him.

Commentary
The theme of how mistaken preconceptions lead to misinterpretation is further elaborated in this chapter. The letter Slope has left for Eleanor is only further proof for the archdeacon of a romantic involvement. Harding's determined fair-mindedness ironically does not help to resolve matters but makes them worse, since he feels he must defend Eleanor's right to choose Slope as a husband and will not discuss the matter with her. This reinforces the archdeacon's convic-tion that he is right. Trollope refuses to see qualities in absolute terms; context must be taken into account. Though Harding does not believe that Eleanor wishes to marry Slope, his desire to be fair-minded is so strong that he cannot act on his belief in case he is wrong, which would therefore compromise his commitment to fair-mindedness. Thus fair-mindedness, normally regarded as a positive virtue, leads to inaction and to the exacerbation of misunderstanding. The archdeacon's character is also seen ambiguously. We see his tendency to read situations in the light of his prejudices and we are told that he is happy only in the company of those who share his views. But these characteristics, which would normally be seen as negative, give him the strength to act with a single-minded strength of purpose that in certain situations is advantageous. Eleanor is like the archdeacon to the extent that she possesses strong preconceptions which influence her interpretations. Thus Slope's familiar tone leads only to a sense of disgust, not to insight into his attitude towards her, since she is convinced her conduct has been blameless. Arabin is involved in these misunderstandings, having been informed of the archdeacon's fears. But ironically this helps to create a romantic liaison between him and Eleanor, as we discover later. The chapter ends with Harding and Eleanor locked in a series of misunderstand-ings of each other based on misinterpretation and false assumptions. For a full analysis of this see the specimen passage and commentary in Chapter 5 below.

Chapter 29: A serious interview

Summary
The archdeacon tells Eleanor that suspicion has been created by Slope's letter to her. Suppressing her indignation, she lets him read the letter and it confirms his worst fears. When she states that she considers it a proper letter to have received, the archdeacon asserts that she must choose between her family and friends and Slope, and tells her that her father, sister and Arabin are agreed that she should not be received at Plumstead as Mrs Slope. Disgusted at this accusation, Eleanor goes to her room weeping. She thinks that Arabin must have been responsible for this idea since those who know her well could never have thought of her desiring such a marriage. She decides to leave Plumstead. The archdeacon still does not realise Eleanor's true view of Slope and informs his wife that Eleanor is proud of her letter. Eleanor sees her father next day and tells him of her intention to return to Barchester. It is agreed that Eleanor will leave Plumstead after lunch.

Commentary
More misunderstanding follows in the interview between the archdeacon and Eleanor, and the narrator's penetration of the minds of both characters allows the reader to savour the ironies of the situation. One is expecting that at last the truth will emerge, but instead we see how difficult it is to resolve human misunderstanding because of the power of preconceptions. Even now Eleanor cannot accept that she has been suspected of wishing to marry Slope and therefore says nothing to disabuse the archdeacon of his assumption, and she irrationally blames Arabin for this accusation. Unlike her father, Eleanor's self-esteem requires that she should see herself as blameless. The narrator reveals the irony that both the archdeacon and Eleanor are disgusted at the thought of her marrying Slope, and though each perceives this disgust, their prejudices prevent them from interpreting correctly its significance. Eleanor cannot believe that the archdeacon could think her capable of contemplating such a marriage, and he assumes that she resents his disapproval of the marriage. Harding also remains unenlightened since Eleanor's self-esteem prevents her even mentioning the subject of marriage between herself and Slope, and his fear of being thought prejudiced prevents him from speaking.

Chapter 30: Another love scene

Summary
Arabin feels depressed at the prospect of Eleanor marrying Slope. He returns from St Ewold's and speaks with her before she leaves She accuses him of slandering her to the archdeacon, but he asserts

his innocence and points out that he only replied to a question put to him by the archdeacon on whether it would be prudent to receive her at Plumstead if she became Mrs Slope. Her reply almost convinces him that she does not love Slope. He follows her into the garden and makes it clear he loves her, but Eleanor, though happy at this turn of events, makes no response because she still feels offended at how she has been treated. When Arabin asks her directly if she loves Slope, her indignation is reactivated and she refuses to answer. She departs from Plumstead without seeing him again, leaving him unsure of the state of her feelings.

Commentary
Here we see that Arabin's romantic interest in Eleanor is serious, but it is ironic and comic that it is his false belief that she is involved with Slope that is responsible for arousing his romantic feelings. Love is therefore seen in a complex context, since it is inextricably connected with various negative responses that Arabin experiences at the thought of a union between Eleanor and Slope. Love does not lead to insight into another person or even into the self. Arabin still suspects that Eleanor loves Slope, and is unaware at first of the nature of his own feelings: 'In truth Mr Arabin was now in love with Mrs Bold though ignorant of the fact himself'. In this chapter the narrator introduces an alienating comment to remind his readers that they are reading a novel: 'How easily would she have forgiven and forgotten the archdeacon's suspicions had she but heard the whole truth from Mr Arabin. But then, where would have been my novel?' Though the novelist may be committed to realism, the reader is not allowed to forget that such realism is mediated through fictional conventions which the novelist manipulates for his own purposes. But realism is not necessarily undermined by such alienating comments, for there are genuine psychological obstacles yet to be overcome before mutual understanding is achieved between these characters, even though he loves her and she realises that he does. Arabin, however, is inexperienced in such a situation and cannot find the right words, and Eleanor's need to preserve her self-esteem is so strong that she must avenge herself on Arabin for suspecting her of loving Slope. She therefore refuses to respond to his love. His direct question to her about her feelings for Slope exacerbates his offence and she leaves him still in doubt on the matter.

Chapter 31: The bishop's library

Summary
When Eleanor arrives in Barchester with her sister and nieces they are told by Mary Bold that the old dean, Dr Trefoil, has had a fit of apoplexy and is not expected to live long. Mrs Grantly hurries to the

deanery. The archdeacon and other clergy have gathered in the bishop's library, adjacent to the deanery, and there is speculation as to who will be the new dean. Slope's name is suggested, which leaves the archdeacon dumbfounded. Dr Fillgrave announces that the eminent surgeon, Sir Omicron Pie, will be arriving from London at nine fifteen. The dean returns to 'a sort of consciousness' and remains in this state for eight or ten days, so that a new appointment does not seem imminent.

Commentary
Though none of the three main suspense-creating elements in the plot has yet been resolved – namely, who will control the bishop, who will become warden, and who will marry Eleanor – the reader can easily predict their outcome. Since the novel is not much beyond the half-way stage, it is time therefore to introduce another suspense element, one which is perhaps more powerful and less predictable than any other in the novel: who shall be the new dean? Trollope does not seek to hide the ease with which the novelist can create suspense in the plot and how that suspense can be manipulated. The dean is placed at the point of death and then that death is deferred. Again Trollope makes the reader aware of novelistic conventions and how the novelist makes use of them. The fear that Slope may become dean is another hammer blow for the archdeacon, even worse than the possibility that he might marry Eleanor. This time the narrator does not inform the reader that this fear is misplaced. We are kept waiting for many chapters before the suspense is resolved. The chapter also shows that human nature finds it almost impossible to focus single-mindedly on death and almost at once begins speculating on the future, in this case on the likely successor to the dean. This topic soon overwhelms the fact that the dean is at death's door. The dean's colleagues' hope that the dean will recover is also not unconnected with their fears that Slope may be appointed in his place. They should not be accused of callousness, however; they are only being human.

Chapter 32: A new candidate for ecclesiastical honours

Summary
Slope informs the bishop of the dean's illness. The bishop has 'aged materially' after a night alone with Mrs Proudie following his rebellion against her. The bishop and Slope visit the deanery. The idea of being dean occurs to Slope. He thinks he could rely on the support of the bishop, Sir Nicholas Fitzwhiggin, who is in the government, and Tom Towers of the *Jupiter*. At the palace, after failing to get any response to his hints, he mentions it directly to the bishop, who is at first astonished. Since the bishop's idea of using

Slope to help keep his wife in check has evaporated and he therefore has no need of Slope, he agrees to discuss the matter with the archbishop. But the bishop makes it clear that Slope must accept that Quiverful will be warden. Slope now feels that his marriage to Eleanor must be settled before she finds out about the wardenship. Her maid has given him an account of happenings at Plumstead which makes him feel confident about his chances. He resolves to visit the Stanhopes only once more. After writing careful and very different letters to Sir Nicholas and Tom Towers, he goes off to see Madeline.

Commentary
In this chapter we see the transition from 'who shall be warden?' to 'who shall be dean?' as it affects Slope. Mrs Proudie's bedroom victory over Slope in the struggle for influence over the bishop ends Slope's efforts to secure the wardenship for Harding, and it also indicates that he has lost the struggle for control of the bishop. His defeat is deferred, however, since he is able to negotiate that the bishop support him for the deanship in exchange for accepting Quiverful as warden, a favourable deal for Slope even though it might make his wooing of Eleanor more difficult. The bishop's rebellion against Mrs Proudie is now over. Even though he is a man of weak character, he can exercise power by using other people as instruments to stand between him and those who may oppose him. But with Mrs Proudie this strategy is impossible, as the narrator makes clear in his comic judgement on the bishop's plan to use Slope as a counterpoise to his wife: 'If indeed he could have slept in his chaplain's bedroom instead of his wife's, there might have been something in it.' After Slope composes letters which reflect his use of role-playing as the means of serving his own interests, the narrator points out that lies and deceit are common under such circumstances. Thus readers who have complacently seen themselves as superior to such a schemer are made to question whether they would have acted any differently. Slope's letters also suggest that no language can divorce itself from rhetoric. He is aware that he must carefully avoid using any rhetorical devices in his letter to Towers if it is to be persuasive with such a man. But this, of course, only means that a more subtle form of rhetoric must be used.

Chapter 33: Mrs Proudie victrix

Summary
A week passes during which the dean lingers on. Slope awaits answers to his letters and Eleanor spends much time with the

Stanhopes in order to avoid Slope. She is still angry with Arabin, though she recognises his love for her. Charlotte schemes on behalf of Bertie but does not realise that Eleanor is too innocent to be trapped. Miss Thorne has arranged a traditional fête at Ullathorne, partly as a welcome for Arabin. Eleanor plans to attend in company with the Stanhopes, but she is not pleased when she finds out that Slope, for whom Madeline has requested an invitation, will ride in the same carriage. Charlotte is pleased at Eleanor's dislike of Slope, since her plan is for Bertie to propose at the party. The bishop returns from his visit to the archbishop the day before the party. Mrs Proudie is angry when she finds out that he has spoken to the archbishop on Slope's behalf with regard to the deanship. She determines to frustrate what she regards as his ridiculous ambition. The bishop's acquiescence with her view earns him a pleasant evening.

Commentary

Though Mrs Proudie is 'victrix', one benefit comes out of the bishop's rebellion: he is able to go on his visit to the archbishop, which she had previously vetoed. Mrs Proudie also behaves more affectionately towards him and exercises less outward domination, but this is only for the purpose of augmenting her power by showing the bishop how pleasant life can be as long as he obeys her. The outcome of the bishop's rebellion is therefore pessimistic as far as he is concerned: Mrs Proudie's combination of assertive power and occasional affectionate behaviour makes her even more formidable than previously. Actions which on the surface might seem to be the reverse of the desire for power, such as kissing, hugging and kind words, are in fact related to it. The bishop in turn adopts a new strategy more suited to his personality than rebellion: complete submission. This results in his disclosing that he has mentioned Slope as a possible dean to the archbishop, thus arousing Mrs Proudie's determination to prevent it, though the bishop gains some pleasure in his mock-innocent surprise that she should not be pleased at such elevation for her former favourite. Eleanor Bold's misinterpretation of the people around her continues in her visit to the Stanhopes, since she is not aware of Charlotte's designs. Eleanor will suffer several embarrassing blows to her self-esteem as a result of her failure to see behind appearances. But though her innocence is disadvantageous in some respects, it does give her an advantage over someone as scheming as Charlotte, since it protects her from even considering any impropriety. Trollope again stresses the moral ambiguity of characters such as the Stanhopes: though open to condemnation on moral grounds, their improper conduct and cleverness make them bright and lively, whereas morally upright people can be dull.

Chapter 34: Oxford – The Master and Tutor of Lazarus

Summary
After Eleanor has left Plumstead, Arabin is introspective. He thinks his love for Eleanor might be partly motivated by her fortune. He also thinks Eleanor does not care for him. The others are as cheerless as he is. Harding is upset over Eleanor's treatment and the archdeacon is worried that Slope may become dean. The archdeacon and Arabin take the view that Harding should ignore Slope's suggestion that he should call on the bishop. They decide they should await the arrival of Dr Gwynne, the Master of Lazarus. Arabin visits Oxford a few days later and sees Gwynne who, somewhat reluctantly, agrees to return with him to Barchester. The Tutor of Lazarus, Tom Staple, thinks it unlikely that Slope will become dean but thinks that Quiverful will be made warden. He concludes that the government might therefore make Harding dean. This idea appeals to Gwynne.

Commentary
In contrast to Slope's confidence that Eleanor will be his wife, Arabin is full of self-doubt. The dangers of the pursuit of self-knowledge are raised by Arabin's introspection. Taken to such extremes, it undermines any positive action. Arabin becomes cut off from his own feelings and is prepared even to acknowledge that he may be acting from the basest of motives. Though Slope is self-seeking and intent on gaining power and wealth by dubious means, he has an energy and sense of purpose which Arabin lacks. Madeline develops this invidious comparison between the two characters later in Chapter 38. In this last chapter of volume two, the Grantly party is at a low ebb. Harding has lost the wardenship, Slope may be made dean, Arabin, the archdeacon's champion who was to take on Slope, is beset with self-doubt, and in addition the archdeacon still believes that Eleanor will marry Slope. The archdeacon therefore turns again to outside help, in the person of Dr Gwynne. But it is not so much Gwynne who turns out to be the saviour of Barchester as the unlikely figure of Tom Staples, an extreme conservative whose knowledge of what is going on in Barchester is highly inaccurate. Nevertheless, his predictions prove to be right and, more important, he puts forward the idea that Harding could become dean, an idea that Gwynne decides to act on. Thus we see once again how chance, in the form of a casual remark, can significantly affect people's lives.

Chapter 35: Miss Thorne's *fête champêtre*

Summary
The day of Miss Thorne's garden party arrives. Slope triumphantly enters the same carriage as Eleanor. He is also pleased to have

received an encouraging letter from Sir Nicholas Fitzwhiggin. He has made up his mind to propose to Eleanor at the party. Mr Plomacy, Miss Thorne's steward, has been in charge of preparation for the party. His main task is to make sure that the 'quality' guests are divided from the others. Miss Thorne is disappointed that her brother refuses to try the quintain, an ancient jousting type of game, so she determines that 'an excellent sample of English yeoman', Harry Greenacre, will act as substitute.

Commentary
The party reveals social divisions. But in the anachronistic world of the Thornes there is a hierarchy which has wide general acceptance and which enables those lower in the hierarchy to accept their place and not feel resentful of those at the top, though there are to be difficulties later. Miss Thorne attempts to re-enact the past, but here there are also difficulties. Her brother refuses to engage in the quintain, and his place has to be taken by someone who, strictly speaking, is not appropriate. She is also unaware that the quintain is not Saxon in origin but Norman. Thus her conservative obsessions are again subject to gentle satire. The first of a number of embarrassments for Eleanor occurs when she cannot avoid having to travel to the garden party in the same carriage as Slope. Though Slope is 'elate with triumph' in this first chapter of volume three, this is the beginning of his fall. Trollope is perhaps suggesting, in keeping with the mock-epic structure of the novel, a parallel with Milton's Satan in *Paradise Lost*. The reader is now in a position to recognise that Slope has failed in two areas in which he hoped for success: he has lost the struggle for control of the bishop to Mrs Proudie, and he has no chance of marrying Eleanor. Only the possibility of being dean remains, and we are not kept in suspense long as to whether he will succeed here.

Chapter 36: Ullathorne sports – Act I

Summary
The early arrivals are reluctant to dance or to eat the food Miss Thorne has provided, and the 'quality' guests are late. The first of these, Mrs Clantantrum, is annoyed because her coat has been dirtied as she descended from her carriage. The Lookaloft family, who should dine with the tenantry, gatecrash their way into the drawing room, which is reserved for guests at the top of the hierarchy. Arabin is disturbed to see Eleanor being helped out of her carriage by Slope. She has had a miserable journey because of Slope's attentions; she at last suspects his motives and wonders whether she was wrong to believe she has not encouraged him. The quintain goes badly wrong when Henry Greenacre falls from his horse, though he is not

seriously hurt. Eleanor talks to her father and claims she could not avoid arriving with Slope. Harding is relieved that Eleanor finds Slope 'odious', but Eleanor is upset since his relief indicates that he thought she may have been willing to marry Slope.

Commentary
The stability of the social balance is undermined when the Lookaloft family refuses to accept their allocated place in the hierarchy. The Thornes are too weak to put them in their place. Mrs Lookaloft's intention to boast that she has consorted with the upper classes will create resentment among those who have chosen to accept their assigned place, and thus will threaten social stability. Even in the protected world of the Thornes, traditional social divisions are being overtaken by modern class differences and the preoccupation with snobbery, status, materialist values, etc. Henry Greenacre's mishap, however, indicates the possible dangers of taking nostalgia for the simpler values of the past too far and too literally. Eleanor is being forced finally to consider whether she herself can be blamed for others believing that she must have encouraged Slope. The misinterpretation theme emerges again when Arabin sees Eleanor being helped out of the carriage by Slope, which his preconceptions influence him to read as a sign that there must be a romantic relationship between them. In Eleanor's conversation with her father, her feelings for Slope are at last clarified without any possibility of misunderstanding. However, openness also has its drawbacks, for when Harding indicates by his delight that he had entertained the thought of Eleanor marrying Slope, this creates a new division, since Eleanor needs to believe that her behaviour was beyond criticism and that no one had reasonable grounds for believing that there was anything between her and Slope.

Chapter 37: The Signora Neroni, the Countess De Courcy, and Mrs Proudie meet each other at Ullathorne

Summary
Madeline arrives late, followed by the De Courcy family, socially the highest ranked guests. The Countess De Courcy blames the state of the roads for their arriving three hours late. She tries to intimidate Madeline with her stare but is outfaced. Out on the lawn she finds a more 'congenial spirit' in Mrs Proudie, who tells her of Madeline's outrageous behaviour. Mr Thorne, though at first suspicious of Madeline, succumbs to her charms. Eleanor takes Bertie as her partner for the meal in order to avoid the attentions of Slope, though she finds herself sitting next to him. From the dining room, she sees Arabin 'hanging enraptured' over Madeline's sofa.

Commentary
Social harmony is adversely affected not only by the behaviour of those lower in the hierarchy but also by those higher. The Countess De Courcy's upper-class snobbery, her inconsiderate behaviour, and her contempt for those of lower status are guaranteed to create resentment. Even though Miss Thorne belongs to an older English tradition than the Norman De Courcys, she cannot assert herself against the Countess and ends up apologising to her. The Thornes are too weak to embody the authority needed to support traditional hierarchy, as is shown by their response to both the Lookalofts and the De Courcys. As Madeline got the better of Mrs Proudie at the bishop's party, so at this party she triumphs over the Countess, highlighting the parallelism between the Thornes' garden party and the Proudies' party in volume one. Unimpeded by any concept of social deference or politeness, and intent on seeing the truth behind appearances, Madeline forces the Countess's pride to suffer a defeat. Again we see the power of the Stanhopes to act positively against forces which pleasant, reasonable, sympathetic people are unable to cope with. Madeline's heartlessness, her egocentric love of domination, give her the psychological assertiveness to overcome the power manifested in the Countess's name, class status, and wealth, behind all of which there is little substance. Madeline recognises this and with her passion for truth is determined not to defer to such worthlessness. She also continues to attract men towards her, and Mr Thorne and Arabin are her latest victims. As Arabin's belief in Eleanor's relationship with Slope was an important factor in arousing his romantic interest, so Eleanor's suspicion that there is something between Arabin and Madeline, when she concludes that he is 'enraptured' with her, increases her interest in Arabin. This illustrates the novel's psychological subtlety, since it suggests that a certain amount of jealousy is necessary if love is to take hold.

Chapter 38: The bishop breakfasts, and the dean dies

Summary
While the bishop says grace at the meal, the dean dies. The narrator informs us that Slope is not on the government's shortlist as his successor. Arabin had hoped to restore his friendship with Eleanor but is disturbed at her arriving with Slope. In his state of misery, he is drawn by the charms of Madeline, who suspects that he is in love with Eleanor. She subjects him to teasing questions in order to confirm that she is right. He admits, however, that Madeline is more beautiful than Eleanor and perhaps cleverer. He is urged into the dining room by Miss Thorne and is given a chair vacated by Bertie, next to Eleanor. Eleanor feels uncomfortable, surrounded by her three suitors, and leaves the room with Slope in pursuit. Madeline has been

impressed by Arabin's honesty and resolves to help him marry
Eleanor and to frustrate Slope.

Commentary

The dean's death creates the opportunity to increase suspense as to
who will be his successor, but the narrator immediately breaks the
suspense as far as Slope is concerned by disclosing that he is not on
the shortlist. As with the earlier disclosure that neither Slope nor
Bertie will marry Eleanor, this allows the reader to observe Slope and
his aspirations more objectively, free from either the fear or the hope
that he might become dean. Again in this chapter continuity of plot is
disrupted by reverting to an earlier situation so as to allow the reader
to see things in a wider perspective. Here we return to Arabin's state
of mind on the previous night and to his thoughts about Eleanor,
when he was in a mental state of confusion and uncertainty. It is in
such a context that he sees Eleanor being helped out of the carriage
by Slope, and this determines his interpretation of the incident as a
sign of a close relationship between them. However, some characters, particularly women, are capable of forming a correct interpretation by sheer intuition. Eleanor did this previously in her
realisation that Arabin loved her, and Madeline does so in this
chapter when she knows instinctively that Arabin loves Eleanor. This
allows Madeline to exercise her power over him. She makes a hurtful
comparison between him and Slope, who is 'full of life and spirits'
while Arabin is 'passive'. However, Arabin's objectivity with regard
to himself and his selfless acceptance of the truth, no matter how
unappealing it might be, disarms Madeline. For example, though he
loves Eleanor, he can admit that Madeline is the more beautiful.
Since he 'had literally been unable to falsify his thoughts when
questioned', Madeline, who normally gains power over men, as with
Slope, by telling them truths they refuse to acknowledge, decides to
help him. Though this appears to be out of character, on reflection it
is understandable. She recognises in Arabin someone who, like
herself, places truth first, no matter what the consequences. With
him, however, this normally creates a Hamlet-like state of mind that
prevents action. But Madeline does possess the resolve and self-
confidence to act and decides that she will take action on his behalf.
Arabin does little for himself in the novel but he is fortunate that
others choose to act for him.

Chapter 39: The Lookalofts and the Greenacres

Summary

There are only two 'little drawbacks' to the success of the party:
Harry Greenacre's fall and the fact that the Lookalofts have dined
with the gentry. The latter is the most serious as far as Mrs Greenacre

is concerned. When she finds out about it she feels bitter. Her husband persuades her to take a more reasonable view. He also persuades Mr Plomacy not to evict a young plasterer, Bob Stubbs, who had not been invited to the party. Speeches are made both in the tent and in the dining room, and there is much enjoyment all round.

Commentary
In this chapter we see the potentially dangerous consequences of the Lookalofts' disruption of hierarchy. Even Mrs Greenacre, who strongly believes in a hierarchical social order, feels resentful and angry, not only towards the Lookalofts but also towards the Thornes. Mr Greenacre, however, it able to take a more balanced view of the situation and any crisis is averted. Greenacre's action to prevent the uninvited Bob Stubbs from being evicted suggests that social relations cannot function harmoniously within too rigid a framework. Also, if there is to be reasonable harmony among different social groups, allowances must be made for the Lookalofts and their middle-class snobbery and the De Courcys and their upper class snobbery. Good social relations are clearly dependent on the existence of people like Greenacre of sufficient character to dismiss the jealousies and resentments that inevitably arise in social interaction. He tries to humanise the concept of hierarchy by allowing it to accommodate an outsider and gatecrasher. His wisdom on this occasion triumphs over Mr Plomacy's tendency to rigidity in this application of the social rules, with the result that the party creates 'universal delight'. However, without Greenacre and his wisdom things might have been very different, which suggests the fragility of this social harmony.

Chapter 40: Ullathorne sports – Act II

Summary
Slope, emboldened by wine, follows Eleanor from the dining room. Despite Eleanor's coldness, he is determined to propose to her. He calls her by her first name and puts his hand round her waist. Eleanor gives him 'a box on the ear', says she will never speak to him again, and runs off back to the house. Though Slope's pride is hurt, he recovers himself and, finding the bishop in conversation with Dr Gwynne, decides to make use of this opportunity to be introduced. But when the news of the dean's death is broken, he leaves at once.

Commentary
The quotation from *Macbeth*, which is a prelude to Slope's proposal, hardly augurs well. However, the inappropriateness of comparing the

murder of Duncan with a marriage proposal creates a mock-epic effect and arouses comic expectations in the reader. Slope has recognised certain signs emanating from Eleanor which on the surface would seem to suggest that she is not pleased with him, but since interpretation is conditioned by prior interests and preconceptions, Slope chooses to interpret these signs in a way that is favourable to his suit. Thus he thinks she might be angry with him because she thought he had been tampering too long with her feelings or that she had not been given the opportunity to confirm that they were going to be married and had therefore to put up with their names being linked in gossip and rumour. We again see the artistic advantages of Trollope's form of narration in this chapter, in the narrator's exploration of the subtleties and complexities of each character's motivation and behaviour and the extent of their misinterpretations and misjudgements of each other. For Eleanor to receive a proposal from Slope is a severe blow to her self-esteem, since it implies that others have been right, especially the archdeacon, in how they have seen her relation to Slope, and that she has been wrong. Even Slope cannot finally fail to see that his suit is going to be unsuccessful, but he has gone too far to draw back. Love, pride, resentment, mortification, the desire to hurt, are all involved in this proposal. The narrator highlights the comedy of the situation by ironic asides, and introduces another alienation effect in shifting from Eleanor's dramatic blow to speculation on the reader's probable disgust at such behaviour from the heroine of a novel. This aside to the reader functions ambiguously in that though it apparently undermines the realism of the situation by reminding the reader that Eleanor is a fictional character in a novel, it can be seen as a means of heightening realism through undercutting the conventional expectations the reader may have absorbed from reading other novels. Trollope encourages the reader to see beyond these conventional expectations to a reality which they exclude or oversimplify. The irony of the narrator's celebration of women as gentle creatures who should never stoop to impulsive or violent acts also questions the adequacy of the female stereotype who tends to be the heroine of conventional novels. The reader is faced with the contradiction between his or her admiration of Eleanor's violent response to Slope's proposal and the fact that conventional morality both inside and outside novels holds that women should never behave in such a fashion.

We again see the power of female instinct in that Eleanor instinctively realises that only such an act could penetrate Slope's defences. Slope's rage is real and understandable enough, but it is controlled and kept within comic bounds by the mock-epic language of the narrator: 'But how shall I sing the divine wrath of Mr Slope . . . ?' Though this experience does not teach Slope charity, one cannot but admire his resilience when, even having suffered such a blow to his pride, he can still seize an opportunity to try to make an impression on Dr Gwynne. Trollope contradicts the reader's expectation that the villain of a novel will be eventually broken and defeated. In contrast, Slope exhibits strength of mind in adversity.

Chapter 41: Mrs Bold confides her sorrow to her friend Miss Stanhope

Summary
Eleanor, upset after her experience with Slope, is relieved to meet Charlotte and tells her what has happened. Charlotte laughs at Slope's humiliation and sees this as Bertie's opportunity to propose. She offers Eleanor the Stanhope family's protection and Eleanor, though slightly worried by the fact that her father is on hand to protect her, is grateful and accepts. They go to look for Bertie and Madeline and find Arabin and Madeline together. While Charlotte and Madeline discuss matters, Eleanor and Arabin hold an awkward conversation. Despite the fact that they are in love, they cannot disclose their minds to each other.

Commentary
Eleanor's trials are not over. She still refuses to accept any responsibility for the situation with Slope, choosing to place all the blame on him. She convinces herself that he is an utterly shameless hypocrite. But in seeking comfort from Charlotte, she jumps only from the frying pan into the fire. Again her inadequate judgement places her in this position. In attempting to justify herself completely to Charlotte, she fails to see that she is being manoeuvred by Charlotte into receiving another proposal, since she allows Charlotte to play the role of protector. What on the surface is a meeting between two women in which one seeks comfort and the other provides it is shown by the narrator to be quite different. One woman seeks self-justification while the other tries to manipulate the situation for her own ends. Neither has any idea of what is going on in the other's mind. The encounter between Eleanor and Arabin is another instance of mutual misunderstanding and non-communication, since both have observed the other behaving in a way which they interpret as suggesting that the affections of the person they love are centred on another. Though they have the opportunity to communicate their love for each other, mental barriers prevent that love from finding any expression. The narrator draws a comparison between Arabin's and Slope's relation to Madeline. But here Arabin's passivity proves more advantageous than Slope's energy. Slope's vows of love, his kissing of Madeline's hand, only lead eventually to his being made a fool of by her. But Arabin's passivity protects him from succumbing in any serious way to Madeline's power.

Chapter 42: Ullathorne sports – Act III

Summary
The guests depart. Harding tells Eleanor that he will inform the
archdeacon that there is no truth in the rumour about her and Slope,
but she urges him to wait. Charlotte and Eleanor eventually find
Bertie, who is told of Slope's proposal. He tells them that Slope has
already left, and though this negates the need for Eleanor being
protected by the Stanhopes, Bertie remains with her. The fact that
marrying Eleanor is a duty for Bertie undermines the attraction he
feels towards her; life in Barchester does not appeal to him, yet he
feels he must obey Charlotte's wishes. Eleanor eventually realises
that she is going to receive a second proposal, though Bertie's
disclosure that it is Charlotte who wants him to marry her indicates
his half-heartedness. Eleanor becomes aware that Charlotte's friendship has been a sham and she refuses to be part of any plan of Bertie's
to deceive Charlotte that he has made a proper proposal. She asserts
that she will have nothing more to do with the family. Bertie arranges
for her to travel home in the carriage with Dr Stanhope, while Bertie
walks.

Commentary
Eleanor suffers several blows in this chapter. Her father's offer to
'undeceive the Grantlys as to that foolish rumour about Mr Slope' is
galling in the context of Slope having just proposed, since it suggests
that her view that she had done nothing to encourage Slope and that
there is no justification for others to think that she has is hardly
credible. She also has to listen to Slope's proposal being recounted to
Bertie. She had thought not only that her relationship with Slope was
perfectly innocent but also that her relationship with the Stanhopes
was not unwise. That judgement is also shown to be wrong when she
receives Bertie's decidedly unenthusiastic marriage proposal. On
being informed of Charlotte's role in this, she recognises the extent of
her self-deception and gains a troublesome insight since 'her mind
was opened to a new phase of human life'. However, her tendency is
still to project blame outwards and therefore her anger is directed at
Charlotte and Bertie. Bertie's attitude to the proposal reveals that a
coherent ethic can exist which is quite divorced from conventional
moral precepts. Though this marriage would give him financial
security and would be regarded by almost everybody as being greatly
to his benefit, it would lead him into a kind of respectability that he
would find stifling. But there is a more important consideration. In
the great majority of novels, love is seen as being reconcilable with
good sense, but for Bertie the latter undermines the former. The
financial advantages of loving Eleanor bring into question the disin-
terestedness of love under such circumstances, and Bertie's devotion
to truth does not allow him to turn away from this problem.

Bertie's attitude to marriage with Eleanor exposes a tension that those who conform to conventionally accepted values refuse to recognise. Eleanor is desirable, 'but the most desirable lady becomes nauseous when she had to be taken as a pill'. The greater the presence of self-interest in any choice one makes, the less one feels a sense of freedom, and if that sense of freedom feels compromised by necessity or self-interest, then love or anything else which can exist only in the context of freedom must lose its savour. Bertie's negative wooing, with its rejection of his own and his family's interest and also of his genuine feeling for Eleanor, implies that such freedom is, for Bertie, the supreme value for which all else must be sacrificed.

Chapter 43: Mr and Mrs Quiverful are made happy. Mr Slope is encouraged by the press

Summary
Mrs Proudie made sure, before she and the bishop set out for Ullathorne, that the bishop confirmed in writing Quiverful's appointment as warden. Mr and Mrs Quiverful call at the palace next day. No sooner have they left the palace than Dr Gwynne calls, having persuaded the archdeacon to let him go alone. Mrs Proudie remains with the bishop and informs Gwynne that Quiverful has been appointed warden. Gwynne leaves disappointed and with a better understanding of the archdeacon's feelings about Mrs Proudie. Slope has received a letter of support from Tom Towers and is pleased to find that the *Jupiter* comes out in support of him as dean. Eleanor's treatment of him still rankles, but though he wishes he could feel the same kind of hate for Madeline, he finds he cannot rid himself of his infatuation.

Commentary
The chapter opens with another move back in time, to just before the Ullathorne party. Two dominant strands of the plot come to a conclusion. It is finally confirmed that Quiverful shall be warden. Also Mrs Proudie demonstrates conclusively that she is the dominant influence over the bishop by forcing him to confirm Quiverful's appointment in writing. This contrasts with Slope's earlier failure to make the bishop do the same with regard to Harding. Mrs Proudie's power is also shown in the visit of Gwynne, another man who vies with her for influence with the bishop but whose civility proves powerless in the face of her dominating presence. His failure to influence the bishop is another defeat for the archdeacon. Tom Tower's support for Slope defers his fall, since it gives him renewed hope that he will be made dean, which is more important to him than marrying Eleanor. In fact, Quiverful's having been appointed warden is some consolation now that Eleanor has rejected him, though any satisfaction is diluted by the realisation that Mrs Proudie has

triumphed over him. His intense hate for Eleanor, even though his Christian religion urges forgiveness, brings out the conflict between Christianity and the forces of human nature. But more hopefully, wilful self-interest and calculation are also vulnerable to those forces, since, despite the fact that Slope is aware that love for Madeline is not reconcilable with his ambition, he cannot overcome his feelings.

Chapter 44: Mrs Bold at home

Summary
Eleanor returns home from Ullathorne tired and unhappy. She reluctantly tells Mary Bold what has happened, since it is painful to admit that Mary was right to distrust Slope and the Stanhopes. She also tells her father when he calls next evening but urges him not to let the archdeacon know. Harding is quite happy at Quiverful's appointment as warden and is intent on staying in his present lodgings, even though Eleanor urges him to live in her house. A letter arrives from Madeline informing Eleanor that Bertie is leaving for Italy, and Madeline asks her to call and see her.

Commentary
Eleanor's self-esteem is subjected to some stress when she has to tell Mary Bold and her father about her experiences at Ullathorne. But there is still no real acceptance that she herself was at fault. For her such an acceptance would seriously undermine her own valuation of herself; therefore she projects hate outwards on those who have been proved right, especially the archdeacon. Her child, however, unable to perceive her in a critical light and unable to deceive, provides some comfort, though the narrator points out the irrationality of such consolation while understanding it. Mary Bold shows character in being able to resist the temptation to say 'I told you so'. But even this restraint is not morally unambiguous, since it is in her own interest to remain on good terms with Eleanor, and exulting in being right would harm their relationship. Harding's similar restraint can be seen in the same terms, since his overriding interest is in preserving his affectionate relationship with his daughter. He makes no reply to her remark that 'It is strange to me . . . that any man should have so much audacity, without ever having received the slightest encouragement.' That Eleanor continues to see Slope as totally to blame suggests that she is so devoted to placing her own ego at the centre of things that virtually nothing will persuade her to take a less self-centred view. Perhaps this 'proud spirit', as she is called in the next chapter, has more in common with Slope than she thinks. Her father also does not hear the whole story, since Eleanor does not tell him of Bertie's

half-hearted proposal or confess how wrong she had been about Charlotte Stanhope.

Chapter 45: The Stanhopes at home

Summary
When Dr Stanhope returns from Ullathorne, he summons Charlotte. He proclaims that he is 'heartily glad' that Eleanor is not going to marry 'so heartless a reprobate' as Bertie. Bertie returns and listens with equanimity to his father's lecture. It is agreed that he will return next day to Carrara and will receive a small allowance. Charlotte is annoyed that Bertie did not make a serious proposal. The day after Bertie leaves, Eleanor calls. Madeline tells her of Arabin's love for her. Though irritated that Arabin should have disclosed his feelings for her to Madeline, she feels joyful at hearing this.

Commentary
Dr Stanhope's indignation has rather an ambiguous effect, since one suspects that he would not have objected if Bertie's plan to marry Eleanor, which he knew about, had succeeded, as this would have relieved him of the burden of supporting him. Thus his moral condemnation of Bertie as a heartless reprobate is somewhat belated. Charlotte's attitude to the failure of the proposal is also selfish, since she sees Bertie's failure to pursue it seriously as a slight against herself. One can argue, then, that Bertie is quite justified in not expressing any remorse for his actions to his father and sister. When Eleanor meets Madeline she again suffers a blow to her self-esteem when she has to listen to a woman, whom she had considered a rival, act as a matchmaker. She experiences a tension between her sense of her own dignity in this situation and her feelings for Arabin. The novel exhibits its psychological subtlety in revealing the conflict between the need to maintain a sense of one's own dignity and personal happiness. Even though Eleanor loves Arabin, she finds it difficult to accept the indignity of Madeline arranging their union. The fact that love nevertheless proves stronger than this need for dignity prepares the way for a happy outcome to the novel. Madeline's request to Eleanor for her not to disclose her apparently selfless action is not without ambiguity. On the surface it would seem to indicate a desire not to take any credit for her action, but it can also be seen as a desire not to wish it to be widely known that she has given way to her heart, which would conflict with the image she creates of someone who is without sentimentality and cynically sceptical about everything. Her devotion to truth is thus compromised by the fact the image she projects of herself is partly a fabrication.

Chapter 46: Mr Slope's parting interview with the Signora

Summary
The day after Eleanor's visit, Madeline holds a small party, attended by Slope, Arabin and Thorne, all of whom are discomfited. Madeline's daughter, Julia, repels Thorne's efforts to be nice to her. Slope is then humiliated by Madeline, who asks him the embarrassing question, 'when is the widow to be made Mrs Dean'? Slope's wit deserts him and he has to suffer her taunts in silence. Arabin must also suffer in silence as he listens to Eleanor being alluded to as the prospective wife of Slope. Slope is now cured of his infatuation.

Commentary
Madeline returns to her original self in this chapter, in which her admirers, especially Slope, discover the perils of their relationship with such a woman. There is something ironic about Slope's discomfiture, for though he is treated cruelly, he also receives the cure for his infatuation that he had earlier wished for. Though Madeline is provoked to attack Slope by his laughing at Thorne's treatment by Madeline's daughter, she does not take any account of others who might be hurt by the way she deals with Slope. Thus Arabin is an innocent bystander who has to listen to the woman he loves being talked of as the wife of Slope. Only a witty rejoinder would be effective for Slope, but the fear that his situation would be even more humiliating if it became known how his proposal to Eleanor had been received renders him silent. Unlike Slope, Madeline does not care that people might view her in a critical light. Thus her gibe that 'It's gude to be off with the old luve . . . /Before you are on with the new' is indifferent to the fact that this could be seen to reflect badly on her. Not caring what people think is part of her strength. However, she is seen in a different context in this chapter in her relationship with her daughter. The child's manner of dress suggests that she is rather a careless mother, ignorant of a child's needs. Julia's disobedience of her suggests that she may give her mother some trouble in the future.

Chapter 47: The dean elect

Summary
There is much speculation in Barchester about who will be the new dean. The archdeacon has many frustrations and worries: that Slope will become dean, that he will marry Eleanor, that Harding will not protest about Quiverful becoming warden. Also, both Arabin and Dr Gwynne appear to have been ineffective, with matters being worse as far as Arabin is concerned in that he has been spending much time with Madeline. Mrs Grantly is particularly concerned at Arabin's

behaviour and thinks her husband made a mistake in appointing a bachelor as vicar of St Ewold's. Harding arrives and informs them that he has been offered the deanship. The archdeacon's jubilation is short-lived when Harding announces his intention to turn down the offer.

Commentary

The archdeacon is at his lowest ebb. Though his strongest quality is his ability to engage in vigorous action against his enemies, he has been prevented from entering into direct conflict with the bishop. He has thus had to proceed indirectly, but his efforts appear to have failed. Arabin has been a particular disappointment. Mrs Grantly's suspicion about Arabin's relationship with Madeline parallels Mrs Proudie's similar suspicion about Slope. The fact that the archdeacon's champion has not engaged in the fight as he had hoped suggests another parallel with epic poetry, since the Greek champion, Achilles, in Homer's *Iliad* also allowed personal matters to come between him and the war against the Trojans. In such a despondent state of mind, the archdeacon is naturally overjoyed at Harding's news, though he ought to know Harding well enough to be cautious. The archdeacon's delight in triumph in conflict leads to his experiencing greater pleasure at the defeat of his enemies than at the good fortune of his friend. Also, since winning is the most important thing, the means by which winning is achieved is less significant. But Harding sees things entirely differently. Confrontation is for him something to be avoided if at all possible. His first duty is not to any personal interest but to the happiness of those dearest to him. His sense of what is right could not allow him to accept the deanship if the appointment was thought to be undeserved. This is much more important as far as he is concerned than defeating the enemy. He does not disguise from himself that his inability to bear criticism is a weakness of his character, and he resists the temptation to judge it as anything else. The novel reveals an unsettling connection between such weakness of character and what appears to be a selfless, altruistic action. In *The Warden* Harding was placed in what for him was the intolerable position of having to bear the attacks of the *Jupiter* while being unable to give up the post of warden without being seen as betraying his church. With the deanship he seeks to avoid at all costs being placed in a similar position. Thus it is difficult to say whether his intention to refuse the deanship is selfless or selfish.

Chapter 48: Miss Thorne shows her talent at match-making

Summary

The following day the archdeacon drives Harding home and makes a great effort to persuade him to accept the appointment of dean. A note from Eleanor awaits him urging him to see her. Before these events Miss Thorne, like Mrs Grantly, had been worried by Arabin's attentions to Madeline and took the view that clergymen should be married. On the day of Madeline's small party she had the idea that Eleanor would make an admirable wife for him and therefore invited her to Ullathorne for a visit in the hope of bringing her and Arabin together. The narrator discloses that she was amazed and slightly disconcerted that her plan succeeded so quickly. Eleanor accepts and goes the day before Harding's visit to Plumstead. Arabin arrives at Ullathorne next day. After some difficult exchanges between them Arabin impulsively proposes and Eleanor accepts him. Arabin and Eleanor leave next day, he going to Plumstead, she to Barchester. The archdeacon is away from home, but Mrs Grantly is overjoyed and believes that this shows that the stories of Arabin's attraction to Madeline were lies.

Commentary

It is interesting that Miss Thorne's matchmaking is less pure in its motivation than Madeline's. It is rumours of Arabin's relationship with Madeline that motivates her to act. Arabin's happiness is a secondary consideration to her belief that clergymen should be married. Her concept of a 'fitting match' is one in which love is unimportant in comparison to more material matters, such as a woman's possession of a dowry. The narrative again breaks with suspense, for the engagement is disclosed at the beginning of the chapter and the rest of the chapter is devoted to discussing how it happened. It is comic that, having been pre-empted by Madeline, Miss Thorne's matchmaking goes almost too well. The pleasure she had expected to derive from watching the success of her scheme is frustrated, again implying that an act which on the surface is unselfish is less so when subject to closer examination. Even when Arabin and Eleanor are almost certain of each other's feelings there are still difficulties. The appropriate language must be found, and Arabin is inexpert. Indeed, how they do end up in each other's arms is left something of a mystery which the narrator cannot explain. Words, with their inevitable ambiguities and associations beyond any specific situation, are seen as a handicap. There is no formal engagement, no promises are asked or given. Mrs Grantly's assumption, on hearing the news, that all the rumours about Arabin and Madeline are therefore false and that they have been the victims of lies and injustice is ironic in the context of what the reader knows. It would perhaps have been more subtle from an artistic point of view if Trollope had omitted the last sentence of the chapter: 'But people in this matter had told no lies at all.' This spells out a point that readers might have been left to make for themselves.

Chapter 49: The Belzebub colt

Summary
Eleanor had not intended to tell Miss Thorne of the engagement but could not help herself. Next day, at breakfast, she finds Mr Thorne and Arabin discussing Thorne's Belzebub colt, an excitable horse. When Thorne leaves to see to the colt, Eleanor and Arabin confirm their love. Harding hurries to see Eleanor after receiving her note and both are eager to tell their news. He is surprised and delighted when he finds out she is engaged to Arabin, especially as he had thought for a moment that she might have chosen Bertie. She tries to persuade him to accept the deanship, but the idea occurs to him that Arabin could be appointed dean.

Commentary
Despite their love, Eleanor and Arabin still have to grapple with the problem of language: 'It was not that she was afraid of Mr Arabin, but she hardly yet knew how to address him.' The language of love is shown as largely a matter of non-verbal signs: 'She uttered no sound, but he could read the affirmation plainly in her face'; 'They neither of them spoke, or found any want of speaking.' Trollope, however, seems to take the usual Victorian view of the woman's role in marriage: 'She would give up the heavy burden of her independence, and once more assume the position of a woman, and the duties of a trusting and loving wife.' In Chapter 44 Harding had wisely concluded that despite Eleanor's experience at the hands of Slope, she would not long be a widow. He is not therefore surprised at her news, but his apprehensiveness as to whom she has chosen, given her previous relationships with Slope and Bertie, plus his determination to accept her choice no matter what, is a pleasant comic moment. The question of the deanship remains. Though the novel is approaching its end, with the reader perhaps expecting that there are no more major surprises in store and that Harding will eventually agree to become dean, Trollope introduces a surprising twist when Arabin becomes a contender for dean. Given Trollope's usual avoidance of unexpected turns in the plot, when he does surprise the reader, the effect is all the greater.

Chapter 50: The archdeacon is satisfied with the state of affairs

Summary
When the archdeacon had driven Harding home from Plumstead, he had been reluctant to believe Harding's assurances about how Eleanor felt towards Slope. He visits Eleanor's house later and

Harding takes pleasure in telling him of the engagement to Arabin. This news creates various conflicting emotions in the archdeacon, but the discomfiture of Slope is particularly pleasing to him. Harding then raises the matter of Arabin's becoming dean and eventually persuades the archdeacon of the merits of the idea. It is decided that he and Harding will seek the advice of Gwynne. On driving back to Plumstead, the archdeacon nearly runs over Slope, who looks as self-satisfied as ever, even though in reality he has just been dismissed by the bishop. The archdeacon then sees Mrs Quiverful at Hiram's hospital and tells her that he is very glad about Quiverful's appointment. He meets Arabin between St Ewold's and Plumstead and offers him his congratulations. He insists he must perform the marriage ceremony at Plumstead, since he is eager to atone for his misjudgement of Eleanor. Finally he greets his wife with great cordiality.

Commentary
Since everything appeared to be so black from the archdeacon's point of view only a few chapters ago, his inability to accept that everything has now turned out well is understandable and also comic, particularly his belief that Eleanor must be mistaken about her engagement to Arabin. The archdeacon finds it difficult to accept that the good can come into being independently of his will, so that the fact that a marriage between Eleanor and Arabin was not anticipated by him slightly spoils this fortunate event as far as he is concerned, but his great consolation is how galling this will be to Slope. Even though events have contrived to work out in such a way as to serve the archdeacon's interests, he needs to feel that he has willed this state of affairs for his happiness to be complete. The idea of Arabin becoming dean is more easily accepted by him even though he had not thought of it, since he will be actively involved in the effort to put this plan into practice. We see another example of Trollope's disruption of suspense when the narrator discloses that Slope has been dismissed, though we shall not find out in detail how this has happened until the next chapter. The narrator remarks, concerning the archdeacon's pleasant greeting of Mrs Quiverful, that since 'things were going very well . . . he could afford to be charitable to Mrs Quiverful'. Ideally, for the Christian, charity should not be dependent on one's own interests being served first of all. There is a clear contrast between Harding's complete willingness to accept Quiverful being appointed warden even though this conflicts with his self-interest. Like his wife, the archdeacon assumes that he has done Eleanor an injustice in assuming that there were grounds for believing that she was going to marry Slope. Neither, of course, has been told of Slope's proposal. If they had, their view that 'Eleanor has had more sense than we gave her credit for' would almost certainly have been modified.

Chapter 51: Mr Slope bids farewell to the palace and its inhabitants

Summary
Slope has had to accept that Mrs Proudie is the dominant force at the palace. He receives a letter from Sir Nicholas Fitzwhiggin which informs him that he will not be the new dean. Looking to the future, he writes to a rich sugar-refiner's wife in London of Evangelical sympathies. He is summoned by the bishop and finds Mrs Proudie there also. The bishop's hesitant reprimand culminates in Mrs Proudie accusing Slope of consorting with Madeline. On hearing that he is to be dismissed, Slope threatens to publish the fact that the bishop is ruled by his wife, though Mrs Proudie is confident that he will not dare to publish anything relating to his period in Barchester, and she is right. Slope refuses an offer to the post of curate at Puddingdale and leaves for London undaunted. We are told that he later marries the widowed sugar-refiner's wife and becomes an eminent clergyman in London. Domestic harmony reigns with the bishop and his wife, for even though he ascends to the House of Lords, he has learned to submit totally to the will of his wife.

Commentary
Now that the novel is nearing its end, the narrator makes sure that the reader does not confuse novels with life. Endings in novels which aim to be realistic must inevitably be unsatisfactory, since the great difference between novels and life is that life is open-ended and novels are not. The narrator also points out to the reader that he is working within the convention that novels end happily: 'we begin to tint our final pages with *couleur de rose*, as in accordance with fixed rule we must do'. The reader is encouraged, therefore, not to confuse a happy ending in a novel with philosophical optimism. In this chapter Slope at last has to acknowledge his defeat in Barchester. But any reader who is expecting that Slope will go down to defeat like the conventional villain will be disappointed. He is already thinking beyond Barchester, and we know from the previous chapter, when the archdeacon nearly runs him over, that he is still defiant. But Mrs Proudie holds all the cards in their last encounter, though Slope does his best to avoid humiliation: keeping her and the bishop waiting, threatening to 'publish the history of this transaction', and, finally, pitying the bishop. He plays his hand as best he can, knowing, however, that he cannot win. The account of Slope's life after Barchester confirms that he remains resilient to the last. This defeat is only a temporary setback. The bishop has also been defeated by Mrs Proudie. Rebellion against her is out of the question and the 'sorrows of a widower's life' belong to the 'millennium'. Men like Slope or the archdeacon could not live with such a degree of domination, but one should remember that it is the bishop's posses-

sion of such attributes as malleability and adaptability that have been responsible for elevating him to the post of bishop and eventually to a seat in the House of Lords. The negative consequence of these attributes is that in a domestic situation he is vulnerable to the power of a strong-minded wife.

Chapter 52: The new dean takes possession of the deanery, and the new warden of the hospital

Summary
Harding and the archdeacon go to Oxford to see Dr Gwynne about having Arabin made dean. Gwynne is persuaded to help, even though he was instrumental in the position being offered to Harding. They arrange the matter after a trip to London, where they have some difficulty seeing the relevant members of the government. Harding and the archdeacon return to Barchester and summon Arabin to see them in the deanery. There is much rejoicing when they finally tell him of his good fortune. Harding is finally persuaded by Eleanor to live in the deanery with her and her husband-to-be. As a final act of good will Harding personally introduces Quiverful to the old men at Hiram's hospital. This helps Quiverful's relationship with those who remember the previous warden and it also enables the townspeople to accept the new arrangements at the hospital.

Commentary
Harding is a strong man when it comes to serving the interests of others, and he allows neither the archdeacon nor Gwynne to persuade him to accept the deanship. However, it is the archdeacon and Gwynne who have to act to put into effect Harding's plan to make Arabin dean. Though the fact that Arabin is made dean is a happy ending, one might, nevertheless, wonder at the system by which such appointments are arranged, with underhand influence being the deciding factor rather than any consideration of the merits of the candidate. One should remember, however, Trollope's opposition to the introduction of competitive examinations to determine appointments in the civil service. The fact that a man like Arabin is appointed without having to submit to objective scrutiny or competition with others implies that there is something to be said for an appointment system that would be seen as unfair by supporters of objective criteria of assessment. However, it can be argued that Trollope departs from realism in having a Whig administration agree to an extreme high church Tory such as Arabin becoming dean. Perhaps we see here how the formal demand for a happy ending can be more powerful than the novelist's commitment to realism. Harding is now a truly happy man, but he has gained nothing for himself. His final act is to make it clear that there is no hostility between

himself and Quiverful and thus to make Quiverful acceptable both inside and outside the hospital. However, whether or not Trollope is implying that Harding is a man who should be emulated is debatable. The narrator suggests that there is something unnatural about a man who desires nothing for himself and identifies completely with the happiness of others: 'He had that nice appreciation of the feelings of others which belongs of right exclusively to women.' Not all women, clearly, as we know from such characters as Mrs Proudie, Madeline and Charlotte. If even women have difficulty in living up to this ideal, how much more difficult it must be for men. Though Harding is admired, therefore, perhaps his qualities are so unique that it would be unrealistic to expect them to be emulated.

Chapter 53: Conclusion

Summary
The archdeacon conducts the wedding of Eleanor and Arabin at Plumstead. The newly-weds then go abroad for a few months. The Proudies leave the dean and chapter to themselves, since Mrs Proudie can do as she pleases in the diocese. The archdeacon is a happier man now that the threat represented by Slope has been removed. Eleanor adopts a more high church position after her marriage. This is the only area of minor disagreement between her and her sister, but Susan Grantly is not worried by this as she realises how bad the situation could have been if Eleanor had married Slope. Arabin returns to scholarship, the Stanhopes to Italy, and Harding continues as precentor of Barchester and pastor of St Cuthbert's, carrying out his duties conscientiously.

Commentary
In this final chapter we have the inevitable happy ending, but the narrator suggests that we should not take it too seriously: 'The end of a novel, like the end of a children's party, must be made up of sweetmeats and sugar plums.' When such happiness and harmony prevail, it is difficult for the novelist to create a great deal of interest. Trollope, however, still provides some pleasant ironical touches. The archdeacon's liberality does not come out of any acceptance or acknowledgement of inadequacy on his part in the past. Indeed, he sees himself as victor, as the epic imagery suggests. Though he thanks God for his triumph over Slope, that triumph had little to do with him. The perfect happiness of husband and wife, which Eleanor and Arabin share, cannot accommodate such a fact as Eleanor's violent response to Slope's proposal, which remains undisclosed to her husband, and it is fortunate that Arabin's marriage vows are not put

to the test by the presence of Madeline. It is fitting that this mock-epic novel ends with Harding, a hero who possesses no conventional heroic attributes but who is none the worse for that.

3 THEMES AND ISSUES

3.1 POLITICS

Central to the thematic structure of *Barchester Towers* is the fact that a community that is predominantly conservative in its ideology finds itself governed by a group of outsiders, the most powerful of whom adhere to an ideology opposed to the conservative one. This theme of conflict between conservative forces who wish to preserve the *status quo* and outsiders who try to effect change is one that can be found in numerous English novels, and perhaps Trollope's treatment of the theme particularly calls to mind Jane Austen's *Mansfield Park*, in which conservative rural values resist and eventually overcome threatening urban values associated with London.

Though this theme is not new, Trollope showed originality in dramatising it within the context of the challenge presented to the Church of England by a movement for reform emanating from within the church. In *Barchester Towers* we see a struggle for power taking place between the Grantly party, high church and Tory in its political sympathies, and the Proudie party, low church and Whig in political outlook. In broader terms, this is a political conflict between an established ruling class and a rising middle class that seeks to displace it. Readers with detailed knowledge of Victorian religion and politics will find the novel enlightening about an important period in English religious and political history.

But such knowledge is not necessary for an adequate appreciation or understanding of the novel. The main concern of the novel is with the general political issues that are raised by this conflict rather than with exploring in detail the particular theological issues of the struggle between supporters of the high church and the low church, though readers interested in Tractarianism or Evangelicalism will find extra resonances in the novel. But the central issue is what happens when a stable structure of long standing – high Anglicanism in Barchester – is faced with powerful forces which desire change.

This is a universal theme in that all structures will eventually be threatened by change, either from within or without. In this case, threatening forces from without have found a place within the structure and, even more seriously, occupy a position of power.

The death of Bishop Grantly, like the death of a king, introduces instability into the system, an instability that becomes dangerous when the new bishop is an outsider who is under the influence of forces who are determined to effect change. Thus the scene is set for a political conflict between those who seek to preserve the *status quo* and those who seek to alter it.

It is well known that Trollope was conservative in his philosophy. But unlike Jane Austen in *Mansfield Park*, his conservatism does not lead to a clear identification with conservative forces in his presentation of the political and religious issues. The narrator's standpoint is essentially disinterested: he observes the conflict between the parties from an analytical position rather than from a committed one. The religious differences between Grantlyism and Proudieism are not explored in detail, since this would be counter-productive to the novel's purpose. The reader would inevitably be drawn into siding with one party or the other and thus would not be able to focus clearly enough on the novel's major concerns: the nature and process of political conflict and how power is won and lost in such conflicts. We see how the Proudie party seeks to use its position of power within the hierarchy of the Anglican Church in Barchester in order to subjugate high church forces and how the Grantly party organises itself to fight back. The narrative standpoint is one of ironic observation of the conflict rather than identification with one position, since the novel sets out to dissect and understand analytically the nature of such political conflicts.

Political conflict tends to polarise opinion so that people are seen as supporting one group or the other. Those who are perceived as uncommitted, such as the Stanhopes, are wooed by both sides. The novel suggests, however, that victory in political struggle is not achieved by one group becoming powerful enough to defeat the other but by one group becoming so weakened by internal division that it is unable to continue the struggle effectively. Both the Grantly and the Proudie parties are internally divided, but the Proudie divisions prove to be much more serious.

The nominal leader of the Proudie party, Bishop Proudie, is not a man of strong conviction and does not desire conflict. The bishop is in the latitudinarian tradition of the low church and has no strong doctrinal views. But he is a man of weak character who is dominated by his wife and her protégé, Mr Slope, both of whom are strongly Evangelical in sympathy. While they remain united, the Proudie party is a political force to be reckoned with.

But shared beliefs are an insecure basis for unity. Both wish to control the bishop, and this will eventually lead to conflict between them and division within the Proudie camp. This fatally weakens the Proudie party and leads to its final defeat at the hands of the Grantlyites. In order to triumph, the qualities of both Mrs Proudie and Slope were necessary. When they begin struggling against each other, their power is neutralised, and when Mrs Proudie finally defeats Slope, the Proudie party is seriously weakened within the Barchester community and has to settle for a much more limited role than it had aspired to previously. There is now no hope of introducing major religious reforms into Barchester, and Mrs Proudie's influence is confined to the diocese. Thus the Grantly party has overcome a serious threat to its power: 'And nothing can be more pleasant than the present arrangement of ecclesiastical affairs in Barchester. The titular bishop never interfered, and Mrs Proudie not often . . . As long as she can do what she pleases with the diocese, she is willing to leave the dean and chapter to themselves' (Chapter 52).

The Grantly party is also divided, and without the much more damaging division within the Proudie party would have been seriously threatened. The archdeacon had been used to being the main power in Barchester when his father, the previous bishop, was alive. He is also a man who relishes conflict. But paradoxically it is the very weakness of the new bishop which frustrates him. For the bishop refuses to allow the archdeacon access to him so that there is little he can do directly to counter the threat presented by Slope and Mrs Proudie. He is forced to rely on others. He enlists Arabin to take on Slope, but finds that Arabin becomes distracted by personal matters and is not the champion of the high church cause which the archdeacon had expected him to be. It would also be an important symbolic victory for the archdeacon if Mr Harding were reinstated as warden of Hiram's hospital, but Harding cannot be relied upon to put the interests of party above questions of personal conscience. Eleanor Bold is similarly unreliable, being vulnerable to Slope's clever flattery of women and too concerned with her own self-justification to act in solidarity with the Grantly party.

It is thus surprising that the archdeacon finally triumphs. But the novel suggests that political battles are not so much won as lost. The division within the Proudie party which eventually leads to Slope leaving Barchester, and fortunate turns of events, such as Arabin being appointed dean, create a complete transformation in the archdeacon's situation. He seems about to suffer defeat on all fronts when suddenly defeat changes into victory. The archdeacon deserves little credit for this, however, for none of his strategies was successful in the way he expected, and his perception and interpretation of the situation have been almost invariably wrong.

Another aspect of the political theme of the novel relates to the Thornes, characters who represent an extreme conservative position. The novel adopts a complex attitude towards them. They look back to an era of social order which is attractive in the light of modern social conflict and complexity. But though their simple social philosophy is shown as attractive and appealing, it is clear that it belongs to a past age which cannot be easily transferred to modern conditions. The fact that the Thornes are the last of their line suggests that their conservatism has value only at the level of nostalgia and can have no serious impact on the present. Though they and their *fête champêtre* are treated comically, there are some serious undercurrents. The attempt to revive medieval practices at the *fête* could have resulted in Harry Greenacre being injured, and the form of class division they attempt to put into practice by having different eating arrangements for the 'upper' and 'lower' classes could also have caused considerable social damage had not someone as sensible as Mr Greenacre been available to rescue the situation that resulted as a consequence of the Lookalofts' refusal to remain in their appointed station. But the Thornes are warm-hearted and genuinely caring people. Their class consciousness is not the product of snobbery or the desire to lord it over others, in contrast to Lady De Courcy, but arises from a sense of tradition and an impulse to protect past values with deep roots from being eroded in the present.

3.2 POWER AND AMBITION

The struggle for power between two parties which constitutes the political dimension of the novel is paralleled by a struggle for power among ambitious individuals. The three most obvious seekers after power are the archdeacon, Slope and Mrs Proudie. The archdeacon's ambition is revealed most graphically in the first chapter of the novel, at the deathbed of his father when he knows that the sooner his father dies the greater his chance of succeeding him as bishop. This situation brings out the power impulse which is normally concealed by social conventions and rituals. The knowledge that his ambition could be frustrated by a matter of minutes creates a conflict in which parental love, Christian ideals and selflessness, and the social unacceptability of admitting to ambitious desires are brought under stress by this power impulse.

There is no simple condemnation of the archdeacon for being vulnerable in this situation, since the novel suggests that the power drive is present to a greater or lesser degree in virtually everyone. He also succeeds in preventing it from overwhelming contrary forces in his nature. Thus the archdeacon's dilemma is seen as a thoroughly human one with which one should identify rather than using it as a means of condemning him for unchristian thoughts. The important moral point is not that he is subject to ambition but that this generates a sufficiently strong sense of guilt to impose constraints on it.

One wonders whether Slope would have been able to exercise control over ambition in a similar situation. But he too is subject to the same tension. He thinks of himself as a Christian, but at bottom the power drive is his strongest impulse, though on occasion he becomes aware of a conflict. What makes Mrs Proudie different from the archdeacon and Slope is that she never recognises that her drive for power may conflict with Christian ideas or altruistic human emotions. Her own power is inseparable from what she sees as the good. It is this absolute sense of her own rectitude that makes her such a formidable figure and too strong an opponent even for Slope.

Slope is the most important of the power-seekers in the novel because he is in the best position to act in order to serve his ambition. He is also ambitious in every area of the novel in which it is possible to be ambitious: he desires effectively to be bishop by controlling Bishop Proudie; he tries to have his favoured candidate appointed as warden; he seeks to marry Eleanor for her money and also to have a romantic liaison with Madeline; he aspires to be made dean. In contrast, the archdeacon has little opportunity to find an outlet for ambitious desires after failing to succeed his father as bishop. Thereafter his efforts are directed at resisting the efforts of Slope and Mrs Proudie to impose their Evangelical form of Christianity on Barchester. Mrs Proudie's power drive is similarly circumscribed. As a woman she cannot achieve power directly since she has no institutional position to provide a focus for her ambition. She is restricted to exploiting the weakness of her husband in order to attain her ends.

What places Slope in a position in which his ambition can take an active form is that by acting as the Bishop's intermediary in his relations with Barchester he can manipulate people and situations for his own purposes. Why then does he fail?

Probably the major reasons are that his and Mrs Proudie's ambition to control the bishop and to take over his authority are in conflict and that Slope mistakenly thinks he is resourceful enough to defeat her. Slope is right to believe that the bishop wishes to escape from his wife's control and would be willing to form an alliance with him in order to do so, but both the bishop and Slope overlook the fact that Mrs Proudie's occupation of the bishop's bedroom gives her an overwhelming advantage.

Madeline's role in the novel shows that power takes other forms than the drive for political authority, high status or wealth. Madeline's drive is for power at the psychological level by making men her slaves. All of her qualities are utilised for this purpose: her beauty, her helplessness as she is crippled, which gives men a false sense of security, her calculating intelligence.

A variation on the theme of power is women's domination. One can see a link between Madeline, Mrs Proudie, Charlotte Stanhope, and Mrs Quiverful. All are able to exercise power at men's expense: Madeline by using her beauty to attract men like moths to a flame; Mrs Proudie by dominating her weak husband; Charlotte by exploiting the laziness and irresponsibility of her father to gain power in the family; Mrs Quiverful by using the force of maternal passion to brush aside her unassertive husband. The first three instances of these forms of female power may be seen as negative, but one could argue that they are the consequence of women having little opportunity to exercise power in a more direct way.

The power theme raises several interesting questions. Does Trollope take the view of certain philosophers and psychologists (Schopenhauer, Nietzsche, Adler) that the desire for power is the fundamental human drive? How does the power theme relate to those characters who are not obviously ambitious or dominating? The bishop is an interesting character in this context. Clearly powerlessness rather than power is his most obvious characteristic. He has virtually no force of personality and is easily dominated. But from a psychological point of view one could argue that this is only a displacement of the power drive. He possesses the kind of personality that cannot tolerate direct conflict with others. His power drive therefore functions to protect him from being crushed by stronger personalities. He resorts to various devices. Knowing he would be outfaced by the archdeacon, he refuses to see him or anyone else who might enter into dispute or argument with him, using Slope as his intermediary. His wife, however, is his main problem, and with her his strategy is submission to her will. When the opportunity occurs to enter into an alliance with Slope and defeat her, he takes it and wins a temporary victory. But when he realises the price to be paid for that victory after a night alone with his wife in their bedroom, he repudiates the alliance with Slope and reverts to submission, even more complete than before.

Power as a psychological theme must be seen in relation to a character's sense of his or her identity. For some people, identity is achieved through the triumph of their will over resistant forces; failure to attain such domination undermines identity and is a serious psychological blow. When Mrs Proudie is temporarily outmanoeuvred by her husband and Slope, this is a shattering experience. She possesses a very rigid form of identity that demands that her power drive always triumph. Her husband's identity, similarly, is vulnerable and fragile. Any threat to his will is intolerable to him, and his method of avoiding the psychological pain of such an experience is either to hide from any form of conflict or else to submit without a struggle to a stronger force.

Harding and Arabin are the two most obviously sympathetic characters in the novel, and like most sympathetic characters in fiction they are not motivated, outwardly at least, by the desire for power or domination. But it would be over-simple to conclude that they have therefore transcended considerations of self. Harding is clearly not selfish or egotistic in the usual sense, but he nevertheless possesses a concept of self which is an intrinsic part of his identity. Basic to his identity is the desire to do what he sees as objectively right, even if this might conflict with his material self-interest. Thus he is quite lacking in any ambitious desire to be warden or dean. He is happy for other men who, in his view, are more deserving to be appointed to these posts. Another aspect of his unselfishness is his conviction that the good and self-determination of others are more important than his own self-interest or personal preferences. He is even prepared to accept with equanimity Mr Slope as a son-in-law if that is Eleanor's choice. Whereas characters such as Slope or Mrs Proudie direct the power drive towards ambitious or selfish aims, Harding's power drive is harnessed to the ideal concepts with which he identifies. Thus it is not so much that he is free from the egotistic force which underlies power or ambition, but that he sublimates it in idealism.

Arabin has several similarities to Harding. His life is governed by a form of idealism that is more important to him than narrow self-interest. In his case this idealism is more negative than positive in that he is not directed so much by the desire to further the good of others as by his sense of truth. He views himself in the same disinterested way as he views others. Thus he is prepared to believe that Eleanor's money is a factor in his attraction towards her. He can discuss his own character in an objective spirit with Madeline and does not reject or resent her unflattering interpretations of his character. However, this commitment to truth makes him incapable of purposeful action to achieve what he wants, even while he recognises that he does desire the good things of life in a material sense. But it is his good fortune that other people who *are* able to act purposefully, such as Madeline, Miss Thorne and Harding, decide to act for his benefit.

Slope and Arabin are parallel characters, and it might seem that Slope is much the more likely to succeed given his powerful ambition, his energy and his calculating cleverness, qualities Arabin signally lacks. But Arabin in fact triumphs over Slope; it is he not Slope who becomes dean and who gains Eleanor's hand. It might be argued that here we have an example of how the formal need for good to triumph over evil which we expect in a traditional novel leads to the undermining of realism. But such a view would be mistaken, I believe. Whereas Slope's relentless ambition alienates other people so that they act to frustrate him, Arabin's lack of selfishness and commitment to truth arouse the admiration of others who then act to further his interests. Individuals, no matter how strong, cannot succeed on their own; they need the help and support of others. Arabin prevails over Slope because he gains such support in Barchester, while Slope either lacks it or loses it. Arabin's triumph, then, does not lack credibility.

In the great majority of novels characters who are not motivated by selfish desires, such as Harding and Arabin, are preferred morally to more selfishly motivated characters, though readers may not prefer them from an artistic point of view. But *Barchester Towers* shows a greater complexity than most novels by recognising that there are negative aspects of Harding's and Arabin's positive qualities. Is Harding right, for example, not to try to influence Eleanor even though he thinks she is going to marry Slope? In situations that call for resolute opposition or energetic action both men are hardly adequate. Even though Harding has the idea of Arabin becoming dean, he could not have put this into effect without the archdeacon and Dr Gwynne. Arabin's self-conscious dissection of his own motives leads to Hamlet-like indecision.

Another indication that the novel looks at unselfishness in a complex light is the fact that the character who is least motivated by narrowly selfish considerations is also the character who is quite unconcerned by ordinary moral standards. Bertie Stanhope is a rootless dilettante who finds it difficult to take anything seriously for very long. Such admired Victorian qualities as moral responsibility or duty are quite alien to his character. He is not a cynic, however, but rather views the world in a spirit of light-hearted absurdity. He is also not amoral but rather acts in relation to his own self-constructed standards. Thus marriage to Eleanor is finally rejected, not because he feels it is morally wrong to marry for money but because the concept of prudence cannot be reconciled with his sense of freedom. No character in the novel is more indifferent to ambition or domination or material self-interest, but no character in the novel is also more indifferent to conventional morality.

3.3 MISINTERPRETATION AND SELF-DECEPTION

The great majority of novels make some use of misinterpretation and self-deception in the presentation of character and relationships between characters. However, it is only in comparatively few novels that this has sufficient thematic force to raise epistemological questions – that is, questions about the nature, scope and reliability of knowledge. Like Jane Austen's *Emma*, George Eliot's *Middlemarch*, and various novels by Henry James, such as *The Ambassadors*, *Barchester Towers* is such a novel, though epistemological themes play a more minor role than in these works. In *Emma* and *The*

Ambassadors, the reader does not know more than the character from whose point of view the action is seen and thus, at a first reading, faces the same difficulty as the character in interpreting ambiguous signs. Trollope and George Eliot adopt a different approach, since their narrators interpret the minds of all of their characters instead of adopting a restricted point of view. The reader is thus placed in a position to observe the characters' misinterpretations and their self-deceptions.

The theme of misinterpretation is centred particularly around Eleanor Bold in her relationships with the archdeacon, Arabin, and her father. All of the latter interpret her behaviour to mean that she has a romantic interest in Slope and is likely to marry him. Their misinterpretations result from the interaction of their preconceptions and fears with an ambiguous set of signs, namely Eleanor's behaviour in relation to Slope and also his behaviour towards her – visiting her, sending her letters, and so on. It might seem that this situation can be easily resolved by Eleanor merely informing her misinterpreters of the true state of affairs, that she has no intention of marrying Slope. But she misinterprets their behaviour as much as they misinterpret her. Because she cannot conceive that anyone could possibly suspect her of wishing to marry Slope, she in turn misinterprets the reasons for their strange behaviour towards her.

Even asking another person direct questions does not necessarily lead to mutual understanding and knowledge. When Arabin asks Eleanor directly what her feelings are towards Slope, she is so incensed at such a question that she refuses to answer, leaving Arabin as far from the truth as he was before. Explanations are also only additional signs which are open to further misinterpretation. Thus what on the surface seems merely a simple misunderstanding that can be easily removed reveals how difficult it is to attain reliable knowledge of other people.

In most novels misinterpretation is completely overcome and all the major characters possess full knowledge by the end of the novel. This is not the case with *Barchester Towers*. The archdeacon and his wife, because Eleanor's marriage to Arabin suits their purpose so well, assume that they must have been completely wrong in thinking that there was ever anything between Eleanor and Slope and Arabin and Madeline. The reader knows otherwise. Though explanations may seem capable of dispelling misinterpretation, a character's need to maintain self-esteem may lead to the withholding of certain embarrassing facts. Thus though Eleanor offers an explanation to her father after the Thorne's garden party, she omits some significant facts – her misjudgement of Charlotte Stanhope and Bertie's half-hearted proposal – and though Eleanor's and Arabin's marriage seems a perfectly happy one, both lack full knowledge of their previous relationships with Slope and Madeline. The reader is therefore made aware both of the inadequacy of characters' interpretations of each other and of the fact that even in the closest of relationships knowledge is likely to be incomplete.

In *Barchester Towers*, as in most novels, self-deception is treated as a moral weakness on the part of the characters. For example, we see that Slope and the archdeacon are so intent on their own ends that they tend to see reality as being identical with their own desires or fears. Thus Slope's desire to marry a rich woman encourages him to believe that Eleanor would welcome his attentions, and the archdeacon's fear of Slope and his general depression about the situation in Barchester lead him to conclude the worst about Eleanor's relationship with Slope on the basis of a few ambiguous signs.

Perhaps self-deception is treated most interestingly in the novel in relation to Eleanor. Here we see the strong relationship between the need to maintain self-esteem and the formation of self-deception. Her need to feel that she is blameless is a strong component of her self-esteem, and she cannot therefore admit to herself that anything in her actions could have been interpreted as offering encouragement to Slope. She cannot understand her treatment at the hands of the archdeacon, and when she realises what he suspects she places all of the blame on him. Even when she finds out that her father also had fears that she was romantically interested in Slope she refuses to accept that her actions towards Slope were in any respect ambiguous. Slope's proposal therefore is a serious blow, since it indicates that there were some grounds for the archdeacon's fears and that her claim to be totally blameless is vulnerable. But her need to maintain her self-esteem is so strong that this knowledge must be repressed, and blame is projected on to Slope who is seen as 'mad'.

Eleanor's self-deception raises philosophical questions about the possibility of attaining reliable knowledge, in that one sees that her desire to maintain her self-esteem is so strong that it places virtually insuperable barriers in the way of adequate knowledge of herself and others. Any potential threat to her self-esteem is either not recognised or else has to be interpreted in such a way that it is reconcilable with the maintenance of her self-esteem. Given that everyone has a need for self-esteem in some degree, Eleanor's case is only an extreme example of a general situation. It suggests that self-deception cannot be seen simply as a moral inadequacy that can be overcome. Human beings can no more entirely eliminate self-deception than they can attain complete and fully reliable knowledge.

The novel does not suggest, however, that there is no point in attempting to achieve adequate knowledge of both oneself and others even if one will never be completely successful. It suggests that one should be aware of and thus seek to overcome the temptation to identify one's beliefs or self-interest with objective truth. Ignorance of such a temptation prevents one from even realising that one may be wrong in one's interpretations or from acting to achieve more adequate knowledge. Yet too strong a realisation that one cannot be sure either of one's own motives or desires and of what is going on in the mind of others can lead to inaction and passivity. Arabin is vulnerable to this form of thinking. Unsure of what Eleanor's feelings are and worried about his own motives in wishing to marry her, he does not act forcefully to win her for his wife and has to rely on the matchmaking of others.

Harding can be seen as the most positive character in the novel, not because he overcomes or is completely free from self-deception but because he avoids the dangers of both the extremes outlined above. He does not project his fears or desires on to reality so that they become identified with it, which is characteristic of Slope or Mrs Proudie or the archdeacon, nor is he subject to the ultra self-consciousness characteristic of Arabin. Harding achieves a truly human compromise between the two. He knows and recognises his own weaknesses and the tendency to impose one's own point of view on reality, and he is aware that others are independent, separate beings whom one cannot know fully and about whom one therefore may be mistaken. But this does not prevent him from acting in accordance with strong principles or from seeking to promote the good of others.

4 TECHNICAL FEATURES

4.1 REALISM

A widely held view of Trollope is that he is the most realistic of Victorian novelists. According to Lord David Cecil in *Early Victorian Novelists* (1934), Trollope's realism is created 'simply by reproducing experience as exactly as possible. He draws always with his eye fixed on his object, never modifying its character, either to illustrate a theory or to improve his artistic effect.' Yet Cecil goes on to assert that this realism is the reason why Trollope is not a novelist of the first rank, since a great novelist 'is not just an accurate observer. Indeed his greatness does not depend on his accuracy. It depends on his power to use his observation to make a new world in his creative imagination.' This shows the divided attitude that critics tend to have towards realism. It is positive in that it is a mark of a novel's faithfulness to experience, but negative when it inhibits the use of the imagination to transcend the world of fact. Many critics' low evaluation of Trollope can be traced to a difficulty in resolving this contradiction.

One of the interests of *Barchester Towers* is that it suggests that Trollope's realism is not the simple, accurate observation of the world that Lord David Cecil believed it to be. Though the novel is convincingly realistic in its representation of character, environment and action, it is also a novel that calls attention to its use of fictional conventions. One is not allowed to forget that one is reading a novel and that certain fictional constraints govern the telling of the story.

It is interesting to compare Trollope with another great Victorian realist, George Eliot. Both use an intrusive narrator who tells the story and enters into dialogue with the reader. Both provide realistic justification for the existence of the narrator by separating him (or her) from the author's real self and making him part of the fiction, in that the narrator claims that his narrative is a story of people who are real for him. Thus Trollope writes in Chapter 4: 'I never could endure to shake hands with Mr Slope. A cold, clammy perspiration always exudes from him, the small drops are ever to be seen standing on his brow, and his friendly grasp is unpleasant.' But whereas George Eliot maintains to the end the narrator's stance as a kind of historian who is reconstructing the lives of real people in the form of a novel, Trollope's narrator often departs from the realistic convention that he is writing about real people and discloses to the reader that the novel is a fiction and that the characters are totally under the author's control. This was an aspect of Trollope that Henry James, in some ways a disciple of George Eliot, particularly objected to as undermining novelistic credibility. The best known example occurs in Chapter 30: 'How easily would [Eleanor] have forgiven and forgotten the archdeacon's suspicions had she heard the whole truth from Mr Arabin. But then, where would have been my novel?' The fictionality of the novel is also stressed by the playful names that Trollope often gives to minor characters, such as Dr Fillgrave and Sir Omicron Pie, a name derived from letters in the Greek alphabet. How can one account for the paradox that Trollope is clearly in a tradition of realism yet undermines it at the same time?

The fact that Trollope wrote forty-seven novels indicates that Trollope was not an innovator as far as the form of the novel is concerned. He was content to work within nineteenth-century novelistic forms and conventions, which enabled him to start one novel as soon as he had finished another, sometimes even the very next day: 'When I was in Egypt, I finished *Doctor Thorne*, and on the following day began *The Bertrams*' (*Autobiography*). If one compares his work with such novelists as Dickens, George Eliot and Henry James, it is clear that there is a greater degree of formal innovation in the latter novelists. Dickens, for example, in *Bleak House* experimented with divided narration, by alternating between omniscient narration and narration by a character in the novel, Esther Summerson. George Eliot in *Daniel Deronda* used a non-linear time scheme in that she started the novel in the middle of the action and then went back in time, and some of the characters and situations seem to belong to romance rather than realism. Henry James continued to experiment with the form of his novels throughout his career.

One important reason why where is continual innovation in literary form is that forms become over-familiar. If writers are to represent reality in a fresh or surprising manner, they must innovate or vary existing forms. The Russion Formalist school of criticism of the 1920s argued that the key to 'literariness' was the use of 'defamiliarising' techniques which had the effect of disrupting the tendency of perception to become habitual or automatic. Writers who were happy to work within accepted conventions without modifying them were seen as being outside literature.

It is clear that the novelist who is committed to representing reality convincingly must avoid merely reproducing forms and conventions that are so familiar to the reader that they are seen as stereotyped. Those novelists who have been seen as major have tended to be those who have been willing to experiment technically or formally in order to 'defamiliarise' the reader's perception of reality and thus to reveal it to the reader in a fresh light. For example, novelists such as James Joyce and Virginia Woolf used a stream-of-consciousness technique to capture a character's thoughts and feelings from moment to moment, and they also radically changed the way time was represented in fiction by making it inseparable from the psychology of their characters. Thus time became subjective, not objective.

Trollope is not an innovator in terms of the form of the novel, but equally he is not content merely to work unthinkingly within accepted forms. An alternative approach to defamiliarisation through formal experiment is to adopt accepted forms but to parody, undermine or manipulate them in surprising ways. This is the approach Trollope adopts in *Barchester Towers*. He makes use of numerous formulaic or stereotyped fictional situations and procedures, but he does not attempt to pretend that they are anything other than that. He draws the reader's attention to the fact that he is writing a novel that operates within the constraints of conventional realistic fiction, but he prevents the creation of a stereotyped representation of reality by mocking and manipulating realistic conventions and formulas. For example, he employs suspense to arouse the reader's interest but undermines it at the same time, as when the narrator tells the reader that Eleanor is in no danger of marrying Slope or Bertie Stanhope. The effect is that formulaic and stereotyped elements of realistic fiction are seen in a defamiliarised context which imbues them with a new sense of reality. This can be shown particularly clearly in the novel's approach to characterisation.

4.2 CHARACTERISATION

Since I have dealt in detail with all of the major characters in the novel in Chapter 3 above, particularly in relation to the psychological themes of power, ambition and misinterpretation and self-deception, I shall focus here on the means by which Trollope creates and maintains the reader's interest in the characters.

All of the main characters of *Barchester Towers* are based on obvious stereotypes whom anyone familiar with drama and fiction will readily recognise: Bishop Proudie is a hen-pecked husband; Mrs Proudie is a shrewish wife; Madeline is a *femme fatale*; Slope is a scheming hypocrite; Bertie is an irresponsible dilettante; the archdeacon is a clergyman more interested in the things of this world than in other-worldly matters; Harding is the traditionally good man; Eleanor the rich widow and Arabin the diffident clergyman are conventional lovers divided by misunderstanding. Trollope also places these characters in numerous situations that will be very familiar to novel readers: situations which give rise to the contest for power or dominance, misunderstandings, several characters seeking to marry the heroine. He takes these conventional elements and situations and proceeds to undermine them by parody or by reformulating them in ways which disrupt the reader's expectations. For example, he places the characters in a mock-epic context by creating parallels between them and the heroic figures of epic poems such as Homer's *Iliad*. The conflict between the high and low church parties is thus compared to an epic struggle such as that between Trojans and Greeks in the Trojan war. This both universalises the struggle for power in Barchester and mocks it by means of the difference in scale between the conflict in Barchester and epic struggles of the past.

One of the main interests of the characterisations of *Barchester Towers* is how Trollope injects a new sense of realism into his stereotypes. A stereotype has its basis in reality, but through repeated representation that relation to reality has been lost. An innovatory novelist may attempt to create characters who are as far from stereotypes as possible. Trollope's method in *Barchester Towers* is to re-invest a sense of reality into the stereotype by having his characters behave, think and act in ways which conflict with the norms that usually govern the depiction of the stereotype. A character like Slope is well known from previous fictional treatments, such as Tartuffe in Molière's play of the same name or Uriah Heep in Dickens's *David Copperfield*. Such scheming hypocrites are usually totally motivated by self-interest and malice and possess few if any redeeming features. Slope, however, is a sincere believer in his form of religion and is convinced that he is acting not merely in his own interest but to further the religious point of view he favours, though the novel strongly suggests that this is a rationalisation on his part. He is also a man of genuine ability, much more capable than his superior, the bishop. Unlike the traditional hypocritical schemer, he sees his own advancement and what serves the good of his religion as inextricably connected and does not believe that he is merely using religion to serve his selfish purposes. One reason way Madeline Neroni leads him on is that she delights in making people aware of self-contradiction. She troubles Slope, for example, by pointing out the inconsistency between his Christian position and the fact that he is wooing a married woman. Whereas the traditional schemer is virtually always completely shattered by defeat, Slope is resilient, able to survive defeat and humiliation. Given his resilience, his later success in London is quite credible.

More complexly, he is a man who is divided against himself, and this is an important factor in his failure. Though succumbing to the charms of Madeline is foolish from the point of view of his other ambitions, he cannot bring himself to give her up. It leads to the disastrous conflict between him and Mrs Proudie and is irreconcilable with his plan to marry Eleanor. Even a man as calculating as Slope has forces in his personality that are not under his conscious control.

The novel's major implied criticism of him is also a departure from stereotype. Normally such characters are condemned on firm moral or religious grounds. But Slope's main failing is that he is not a gentleman. The concept of the gentleman as a kind of spiritual ideal is an important one for Trollope, though he was reluctant to define it. It is related to the traditional idea of rank, though it is not identified with it, since many men who were gentlemen in terms of rank lacked the spiritual qualities associated with it. The true gentleman, for Trollope, was a man of principle and honour, but these qualities came from the heart rather than from conscious reflection. Money and education on their own were not capable of developing such qualities. Thus Slope, who has not been born to gentlemanly status though he has acquired a gentlemanly veneer, lacks true gentlemanly feeling. It is suggested that this is at the root of his lack of principle, his unbridled individualism, his contempt for past values and tradition. (For a fuller discussion of this, see the book by Robin Gilmour listed in 'Further Reading'.)

Similarly, the stereotype of the dominating wife is defamiliarised by Trollope's treatment of Mrs Proudie. She is a woman of strong personality, but since, as a woman, her energies cannot find any direct expression through playing some acceptable social role, it is natural that she should seek power indirectly through her husband. One should also see her dominating qualities in relation to her husband's fear of confrontation. Because he adopts a policy of non-resistance, her dominating qualities are subject to no control whatsoever. The weakness of her husband can also be seen as a factor in making her take an interest in Slope, though she sees her relationship to him as a purely religious one. But her moral disapproval of Madeline, who attracts her protégé away from her, can be interpreted as being unconsciously motivated by jealousy. A scene such as the one in which she is out-manoeuvred by Slope and her husband and has to accept defeat also exposes complexities in her character that go beyond the stereotype of the dominating wife. She has become so used to having her own will that this defeat is a blow to her identity, especially since she will have to tell Mrs Quiverful that she has failed. But she is not merely thinking of herself, for she had been genuinely moved by Mrs Quiverful's plight and had wanted to help her. Her defeat therefore is a double blow. But whereas the stereotypical dominating wife is usually broken by defeat, Mrs Proudie fights back and becomes more dominating than ever both by asserting her power in the bedroom and by making it clear to her husband that he will be rewarded with a pleasant life as long as he does what she wants.

Other notable instances of departure from stereotype are Madeline's altruistic impulse to act to bring together Arabin and Eleanor, when the conventional *femme fatale* would have seized the opportunity to exploit the situation for her own benefit; the carefree and previously irresponsible Bertie's discovery that certain principles do govern his life when he finds that he cannot bring himself to marry Eleanor for her money; Harding's determination to be fair and just ironically preventing understanding taking place between him and Eleanor and worsening relations between her and the Grantlys; the conventional love relationship between Arabin and Eleanor being partly provoked by his jealousy of Slope and her jealousy of Madeline and also raising general philosophical problems concerning interpretation and knowledge.

4.3 NARRATION

One of the major differences between Victorian and twentieth-century fiction is that in the former, predominantly, the story is recounted by a narrator who draws attention to himself as storyteller and who intervenes to comment on the action and on the characters, often moralistically, while in the latter the narrator has given way to narration in which there is no personalising of the narrator, unless the novel is narrated in the first person. The narrator is especially prominent in *Barchester Towers*: 'This narrative is supposed to commence immediately after the installation of Dr Proudie. I will not describe the ceremony as I do not precisely understand its nature. I am ignorant whether a bishop be chaired like a member of parliament, or carried in a gilt coach like a lord mayor' (Chapter 3). Until fairly recently this intrusive form of narration was seen by many critics as an artistic weakness of Victorian fiction. Such critics argued that the novelist should 'show' rather than 'tell'. As Percy Lubbock writes in *The Craft of Fiction* (1921): 'the art of fiction does not begin until the novelist thinks of his story as a matter to be *shown*, to be so exhibited that it will tell itself'.

In recent years this view has been questioned, partly because certain modern novelists have made use of Victorian modes of narration, and also because theorists of the novel have viewed the intrusive narrator of Thackeray, Trollope and George Eliot as an artistic device that should be understood in its own terms rather than being attacked as artistically inferior.

One important reason why critics preferred 'showing' to 'telling' was that they took the view that the literary work should be an organic structure that was completely self-contained. The art of the novel was undermined if attention was directed either to author or reader. Structure in the novel was perceived in spatial terms, that is, all elements of the work should cohere within one temporal plane, like a painting or a piece of sculpture. This artistic ideal was difficult to reconcile with the presence of an intrusive narrator who addressed the reader, interrupted the action with digressions, and made moral or philosophical comments, all of which seemed to offend against an organic or spatial concept of structure. But it can be argued that artistic form can accommodate the anti-dramatic techniques used by such novelists as Trollope or George Eliot in which the narrator enters into a kind of relationship with the reader. Without this interplay between narrator and reader, which gives the novelist great scope to use and manipulate the reader's expectations, *Barchester Towers* would be a much less interesting and entertaining novel.

This unsettling or destabilisation of the reader's expectations has both an artistic and a moral function. Predictable situations or familiar character types give the novelist scope to introduce surprising variations or departures from the norm so that reality is represented in a defamiliarised manner which renews the reader's perceptions. This also has a moral effect in that the undermining of stereotyped responses discourages unthinking or bigoted or prejudiced judgements. The narrator plays an essential role in this process since he is in continual dialogue with the reader, often encouraging the reader to respond to a situation with conventional attitudes, only to undercut these. Thus in Chapter 1 the narrator appears to be condemning the archdeacon in orthodox moral terms which the reader can readily agree with, since the archdeacon, though a man of religion, cannot forget about his personal ambition in spite of the fact that his father is on his deathbed. But at the end of the chapter the narrator suddenly cuts the ground from this point of view by defending the archdeacon and implicitly reproving the reader for being tempted by an easy moral condemnation based on an unrealistic view of clergyman as being above normal human emotions.

The narrator's manipulation of suspense is another example of an interplay with the reader that has both artistic and moral effects. Trollope believed that suspense was an artistically objectionable aspect of novels, as he makes clear in Chapter 15. Wondering what is going to happen next is clearly a distraction from what might be seen as the more important elements of the novel, such as complexities of motivation, moral dilemmas, social or psychological analysis. But if suspense is completely discarded, this creates the problem for the novelist of maintaining the reader's interest. Trollope uses the intrusive narrator to help him overcome this problem. The narrator's interventions allow Trollope's concern about suspense as an artistic device to become incorporated into the novel's structure and content. The best known disruption of suspense occurs when the narrator informs the reader that there is no danger of Eleanor marrying Bertie or Slope. In itself this is a shock, since most novels are built around keeping the reader in doubt about such matters. It is therefore defamiliarising in formal terms since it undermines conventional narrative expectations. The narrator, however, does not disclose whom she will marry, which retains an element of suspense, but, more important, the reader is now in a position to perceive Eleanor's relations with Slope and Bertie in a more disinterested and critical spirit. The humour of these relations can be more readily appreciated without the fear that Eleanor may marry one of these men, and Eleanor can also be viewed in a more critical light.

The form of narration associated with Victorian novelists such as Trollope is often called 'omniscient'. This term is unfortunate because it suggests that the narrator is a god-like figure who possesses such superhuman attributes as omniscient knowledge of the world and of other people's minds. Modern narrative techniques which assume that knowledge is subjective, partial or limited and which structure their narratives on this basis are often therefore seen as superior to Victorian narrative practice.

But there is no necessary contradiction between so-called 'omniscient' narration and the belief that knowledge is subjective, partial or limited. Victorian narrators tend to compare themselves to historians or biographers. In Chapter 20 of *Barchester Towers*, the narrator writes: 'How often does the novelist feel, ay, and the historian also and the biographer, that he has conceived within his mind and accurately depicted on the tablet of his brain the full character and personage of a man, and that, nevertheless, when he flies to pen and ink to perpetuate the portrait, his words forsake, elude, disappoint, and play the deuce with him'. The narrator's knowledge of other minds does not imply that he possesses superhuman attributes; it is best seen as imaginative construction and interpretation, just as a historian might try to penetrate the minds of historical figures. Historiography was one of the most important cultural manifestations of the nineteenth century, and the historical novel was a nineteenth-century invention. This had an impact on the non-historical novel, for the detached, disinterested and critical perspective which a historian adopted towards the past could also be adopted towards the present. Victorian narrators are more usefully seen as resembling historians than as god-like figures.

However, Henry James's objection to Trollope's narrator's admission that the novel was 'a make-believe' was based on the fact that this undermined the narrator's role as historian: 'It is impossible to imagine what a novelist takes himself to be unless he regard himself as an historian and his narrative as a history.' But James's implicit assumption that the historian's work directly reflects reality is questionable. Historians cannot avoid having to construct narratives to contain the real people and events which they judge important and significant enough to constitute history. But such narrative structuring is as fictional as the narrative structuring of a novel; that is, it is not a part of the world but something made by the historian. One might be startled, as James points out, if a historian 'were to drop the historic mask and intimate that William of Orange was a myth or the Duke of Alva an invention', but there is no reason why one should be shocked if a historian pauses to point out that the narrative he has created to include such figures and his interpretation of them is fictional, in other words an imaginative construction, in that quite different narratives which embodied opposed interpretations of these historical figures are possible.

Modern theorists of the novel have seen the novel as being divided between 'story' and 'discourse', 'story' being the basic material of the fiction, such as characters, what happens and where is happens, while 'discourse' is the organisation of this material into the form of a novel. The form of narration adopted, the narrative structure, the use of symbolism and imagery, the implicit attitude of the author towards his material would all come under the general heading of 'discourse'. This implies that the same basic story can be narrated in an infinite number of ways. A similar division exists in historical narrative. Though there was only one Napoleon and Battle of Waterloo, there is no limit to how they can be interpreted and constructed in historical narratives.

The narrator of *Barchester Towers*, like a historian, is engaged in a task of construction and interpretation. It is clear that a character such as Mr Slope is being judged from a particular viewpoint, but by implication other interpretations of Slope are possible. Of course, the difference between the novelist and the historian is that, unless the novel uses historical characters, its narrative is invented, whereas historical narrative uses data which have an independent existence. As I have argued above, this distinction is less radical than one might think, and in any case virtually all novels include a great deal of historical data. Theoretically, however, the reader of a historical narrative has independent access to the historian's sources, whereas a reader of a novel has to accept the novelist's 'story' as given. But both the novelist and the historian have to submit to the same test. They must persuade the reader that their constructions and interpretations of their material are convincing. In addition, the novelist must be entertaining and interesting.

In some nineteenth-century novels, the story/discourse distinction was thematicised, that is, made part of the novel's thematic structure.

In Emily Brontë's *Wuthering Heights*, for example, the same set of events is narrated from several different points of view, so that the reader is encouraged to speculate about such matters as the relation between how a character sees and interprets events and that character's underlying interests or prejudices. Some novels narrated in the third person, such as George Eliot's *Middlemarch*, can also be seen as incorporating point of view and interpretation in the thematic structure, by making the reader aware of the fact that the narrator's viewpoint is governed by certain interests, assumptions and beliefs. This viewpoint can therefore claim to be only an interpretation. By implication, other interpretations are possible. Though, as I suggested earlier, *Barchester Towers* is concerned with point of view and interpretation, there is little attempt to thematicise the relation between 'story' and 'discourse', narrator and his narration, in the same way. It is clear that the narrator is shaping his story and judging his characters from a particular viewpoint, but we are not encouraged, as I believe we are in *Middlemarch*, to reflect on the narrator's interpretative processes.

Trollope's narration is also more flexible than it might appear to be on the surface. A device which has become increasingly common in fiction is the 'indirect free style', by which a novelist can move from external description or commentary to representation of a character's thoughts or point of view without pausing to say 'he thought' or 'she said to herself'. More experimental modern novelists go beyond this and use stream-of-consciousness techniques which attempt to capture a character's thoughts and feelings in operation. Trollope's or George Eliot's form of narration inhibits a thoroughgoing use of such techniques, which are especially appropriate in dramatising introverted or passive characters. But the intrusive narrator of these novelists is capable of moving from direct commentary to something like identification with a character's mind, on occasion in a manner akin to the indirect free style. One sees this in *Barchester Towers* when Trollope explores a character in detail, such as Slope in Chapter 4 or Arabin in Chapter 20. Trollope's style of narration in the novel is not therefore irreconcilable with a more inward representation of character, even if it cannot explore mental processes or the workings of the unconscious as thoroughly as modern novelists.

But all literary techniques have built-in advantages and limitations. The great advantage of Trollope's style of narration is that it allows the novel to range over the whole of a society and deal with a wide spectrum of characters. The modern novel, in exploring consciousness in depth, has sacrificed to a considerable extent the social breadth of Victorian fiction. Trollope's narrator moves freely from one social group to another, penetrates the consciousness of dozens of characters, actively involves the reader through direct address or irony, reveals the complexities of the interactions between and among characters by being able to show how they fail to understand or misjudge each other. The narrator is one of the main components of Trollope's fiction and one of its major artistic successes.

4.4 LANGUAGE AND STYLE

Of all the major English novelists of the nineteenth century, Trollope seems least noteworthy in terms of his language and style. Dickens's power of imagination, Thackeray's satirical wit, George Eliot's intellectual scope, make their works distinctive in style and language. In comparison, the texture of Trollope's fiction appears to be mundane. Indeed, some critics have denied that he has any style at all. Lord David Cecil writes:

> But it is in his style that Trollope's relative weakness of imagination shows itself most clearly. Style is the writer's power to incarnate his creative conceptions in a sensible form. And all the great writers have a very marked style . . .
>
> Now of style, in this sense, Trollope has none at all. He writes easily and unaffectedly – and his tone of voice has its own masculine friendliness. But that is all. He has no characteristic cadence, no typical unique use of image and epithet; even at his best we feel we could paraphrase him without losing anything essential to his flavour.

This view of style, however, assumes that it exists as something separate from a work's other qualities and characteristics. Cecil does not consider the possibility that Trollope did not wish to have a literary style that would draw attention to itself. It seems certain that Trollope deliberately set out to avoid fine writing. In a letter to George Eliot he wrote: 'I have shorn my fiction of all romance.' His realistic project entailed that his language be as unobtrusive as possible. The less the reader noticed the language and style of his novels, the more powerful was the sense of reality created.

But this does not mean that his novels have no style or that there is nothing of interest to say about his language. Rather, their plainness of language, with their relative simplicity of sentence structure and straightforward diction, their avoidance of metaphor and obvious literary devices, represent a stylistic choice on Trollope's part. He had to work hard to achieve the effect of creating a representation of reality in which words seem to play no significant mediating role. Indeed, one can see a parallel between Trollope as stylist and Mr Slope in the letter he writes to Tom Towers in Chapter 32. Slope knows that Towers will see through flattery and will be offended at any obvious attempt to persuade him to support his aspiration to be dean. Slope must therefore use all his power of rhetoric precisely to conceal his letter's persuasive aim:

> this letter must, in appearance at least, be written without effort, and be fluent, unconstrained, and demonstrative of no doubt or fear on the part of the writer. Therefore the epistle to Mr Towers was studied, and recopied, and elaborated at the cost of so many minutes, that Mr Slope had hardly time to dress himself and reach Dr Stanhope's evening.

Trollope's realistic art conceals a similar rhetorical control over language. His purpose is to make his style so apparently non-existent that the reader will be unconscious of its presence and so be totally persuaded by its realism. But this effect is achieved by linguistic means, and Trollope's awareness of this suggests that he writes with a degree of linguistic and stylistic self-consciousness for which critics such as Lord David Cecil do not give him credit.

An especially notable aspect of Trollope's use of language is his dialogue. Virtually all of his characters speak in a distinctive way which is appropriate to their personalities. This is another important element of Trollope's realism, since it indicates that he allows his characters to have a separate existence and to speak for themselves. They do not appear to be mere puppets under the total control of a puppet-master.

If one looks at some scenes in the novel one sees that the major characters use language in distinctive ways which throw light on their personalities. In the scene in which the archdeacon and Harding visit Bishop and Mrs Proudie for the first time, Mrs Proudie's overbearing personality comes out in the language she uses, particularly her effort to achieve rhetorical emphasis by her repetition of 'surely': 'But surely, Dr Grantly . . . surely we should look at it differently. You and I, for instance, in our position: surely we should do all that we can to control so grievous a sin' (Chapter 5). In contrast, the bishop will always try to avoid direct statement and favours such phrases as 'upon the whole' and 'might have'. There is a similar contrast between the speech of the archdeacon and Harding. The archdeacon's outraged 'Good heavens!' and his violence of language – 'He [Slope] is the most thoroughly bestial creature that ever I set my eyes upon' (Chapter 6) – contrasts with Harding's more measured language: 'I can't say I felt myself much disposed to like him.'

This contrast between different types of speech enhances the interest of many of the encounters between the characters. In Harding's interview with Slope in Chapter 12 one sees how Slope's surface politeness masks a desire to manoeuvre Harding into doing what he wants: 'I believe, if I am rightly informed, there can hardly be said to have been any duties hitherto', and he invokes the bishop when he wishes to say something which he knows Harding will find particularly offensive: 'I hope, however, you fully understand the bishop's wishes about the new establishment of the hospital; and if, as I do not doubt, I shall receive from you an assurance that you accord with his lordship's views, it will give me very great pleasure to be the bearer from his lordship to you of the presentation to the appointment.' But Harding counters Slope's elaborate sentences with straightforward questions that disconcert Slope: 'But if I disagree with his lordship's views?'; 'But if I accept the appointment, and yet disagree with the bishop, what then?'

Episodes such as the Proudies' evening party and the Thornes' garden party give Trollope particular scope to exploit his skill with dialogue. Indeed, there is a dramatic quality about these scenes such that if all narrative commentary was excluded leaving only the dialogue, one would still have a strong sense of the different characters and of the comedy of the scenes. At the Proudie reception, for example, Bertie Stanhope's free and easy conversation, with its colloquialisms and direct questions, is in marked contrast to the formal and impersonal language of the bishop and such artificialities as Mrs Proudie's 'Unhand it, sir!'

Yet Trollope also avoids the Dickensian approach to speech by which the linguistic attributes of the characters recur virtually every time they appear, as with such figures as Mr Micawber in *David Copperfield* or Flora Finching in *Little Dorrit*. Such highly stylised speech would have offended against Trollope's type of realism. Though his characters use language in a way which is distinctive and characteristic, they are not defined by their language in the way that Micawber or Flora Finching are. His first priority is to suggest that beyond the language the characters use is a human consciousness.

5 SPECIMEN PASSAGE

AND

COMMENTARY

5.1 SPECIMEN PASSAGE (CH. 28)

How hard it is to judge accurately the feelings of others. Mr Harding, as he came to the close of the letter, in his heart condemned his daughter for indelicacy, and it made him miserable to do so. She was not responsible for what Mr Slope might write. True. But then she expressed no disgust at it. She had rather expressed approval of the letter as a whole. She had given it to him to read, as a vindication for herself and also for him. The father's spirits sank within him as he felt that he could not acquit her.

And yet it was true feminine delicacy of Eleanor's mind which brought on her this condemnation. Listen to me, ladies, and I beseech *you* to acquit her. She thought of this man, this lover of whom she was so unconscious, exactly as her father did, exactly as the Grantlys did. At least she esteemed him personally as they did. But she believed him to be in the main an honest man, and one truly inclined to assist her father. She felt herself bound, after what had passed, to show this letter to Mr Harding. She thought it necessary that he should know what Mr Slope had to say. But she did not think it necessary to apologize for, or condemn, or even allude to the vulgarity of the man's tone, which arose, as does all vulgarity, from ignorance. It was nauseous to her to have a man like Slope commenting on her personal attractions; and she did not think it necessary to dilate with her father upon what was nauseous. She never supposed they could disagree on such a subject. It would have been painful for her to point it out, painful for her to speak strongly against a man of whom, on the whole, she was anxious to think and speak well. In encountering such a man she had encountered what was disagreeable, as she might do in walking the streets. But in such encounters she never thought it necessary to dwell on what disgusted her.

And he, foolish, weak, loving man, would not say one word, thought one word would have cleared up everything. There would have been a deluge of tears, and in ten minutes everyone in the house would have understood how matters really were. The father would have been delighted. The sister would have kissed her sister and begged a thousand pardons. The archdeacon would have apologized and wondered, and raised his eyebrows, and gone to bed a happy man. And Mr Arabin – Mr Arabin would have dreamt of Eleanor, have awoke in the morning with ideas of love, and retired to rest the next evening with schemes of marriage. But, alas, all this was not to be.

Mr Harding slowly folded the letter, handed it back to her, kissed her forehead and bade God bless her. He then crept slowly away to his own room. (Penguin edition, pp. 265–6)

5.2 COMMENTARY

Eleanor has given Mr Harding Slope's letter to her to read. She expects that, when he discovers that the way is apparently clear for him to return as warden to Hiram's hospital, he will be pleased and that her dealings with Slope, so disapproved of by the archdeacon and her sister, will be justified. She is disappointed, however, for Harding resents Slope's interference on his behalf and dislikes even more his intimate tone of address to Eleanor. He concludes that Eleanor must have encouraged Slope for him to write in such a manner.

Having presented Harding's interpretation of Slope's letter, the narrator draws the conclusion that it illustrates the difficulty of understanding another's feelings. This is the kind of general comment which Trollope's narrator habitually makes and which readers unsympathetic to this form of narration often see as undramatic, moralistic, or gratuitous. But in fact the narrator is drawing the reader's attention to one of the novel's major thematic concerns: misinterpretation and the difficulty of knowing what is going on in the mind of another person. The narrator then returns to presenting Harding's view of the situation in terms that are close to how Harding might have considered the matter in his own mind: 'She was not responsible for what Mr Slope might write. True. But then she expressed no disgust at it.'

Harding's misinterpretation of how Eleanor feels about Slope is particularly significant, since it is not misinterpretation founded on projection or prejudice on his part. He is eager to be as fair and just to Eleanor as possible, and would gladly give her the benefit of any doubt. There is no more fair-minded person in the novel, and probably in all English fiction, than Mr Harding. Yet he still misinterprets Eleanor's feelings for Slope. This shows the difficulty of knowing what is going on in the mind of another, since even a man like Mr Harding, who does everything in his power to appreciate the other person's point of view, misjudges his own daughter.

In the next paragraph the narrator switches from identification with Harding's point of view to direct address to the reader: 'Listen to me, ladies, and I beseech *you* to acquit her.' It might be argued that this direct address to his women readers is a typical piece of self-indulgence on the part of Trollope's narrator. But this appeal to the woman reader has its point. Harding misjudges how his daughter feels because, as a man, he does not or cannot think of the situation from the woman's point of view. Even such a fair-minded man is unable to appreciate 'the true feminine delicacy of Eleanor's mind'. The narrator then presents Eleanor's point of view. She is as aware of the vulgarity of Slope's tone as her father, but she assumes that he will know how she feels about it and that there is, therefore, no necessity for her to point this out. Indeed, if she did express her disgust at Slope's tone this would be an implicit admission that she believed that her father might have thought that she did not feel such disgust. Since she feels certain that he will know how she feels, she ignores Slope's offensive tone and concentrates on what she considers the more important matter – Slope's news that her father will be appointed as warden – and she assumes that her father will do the same.

Another factor which makes it difficult for Eleanor to refer to the offensiveness of Slope's personal remarks is that, as a woman, she has a distaste for mentioning or pointing out anything that she considers 'nauseous' or 'disgusting'. This is something that only another woman, or a novelist able to identify with the woman's point of view, is likely to appreciate. Men will tend to find this extreme sensitivity difficult to understand, but one of the things the narrator is doing is giving his male readers an insight into the otherness and therefore strangeness of women. This has both an artistic and moral effect on the reader in that it represents the female sensitivity as radically different from the male and thus presents an aspect of reality in a fresh and interesting light; it also encourages male readers to move beyond the limitations of their viewpoint and recognise the otherness of a female point of view.

In the next paragraph the narrator returns to Harding's point of view. He possesses a different kind of delicacy from that of Eleanor which prevents the misunderstanding being resolved. Determined not to impose his opinions and judgements on another person, he makes no comment that would betray what he thinks of Slope's letter. Since they both remain locked in their false interpretations of each other, they are caught up in a network of mutual misunderstanding and misjudgement. One word would have cleared up matters and restored everyone to happiness, 'But, alas', says the narrator, 'all this was not to be'. This is a Hardy-like touch, since the cause of the characters' misery is made to seem trivial and slight: the non-utterance of one word. Victorian novelists are especially sensitive to the fact that what on the surface seems trivial, a word not spoken, a letter being pushed under a carpet – as in Hardy's *Tess of the d'Ubervilles* – can produce potentially tragic effects out of all proportion to the triviality of the cause. Many modern readers dislike such effects and often dismiss them as contrivances, but perhaps a deeper reason for this dislike is a reluctance to face the underlying philosophical point that human lives can be ruined by trivial mischances.

The narrator's 'alas' is ambiguous in this context. Emphasis is placed on the catalogue of misfortune which results from Harding's and Eleanor's failure to understand each other's feelings. The narrator is assuming that the reader will possess sufficient human feeling and morality to regret the fact that these characters are deprived of happiness. But, of course, this is a novel, and if that one word had been uttered and misunderstanding had been overcome and happiness all round had ensued, there would be no more novel. As the narrator remarks in a similar situation in Chapter 30, when misunderstanding between Eleanor and Arabin might have been resolved by one of them taking the initiative: 'But then, where would have been my novel?' This comment implicitly applies to this earlier situation.

Both the narrator as novelist and the reader of novels are in a similarly ambiguous position. Both must, as moral beings, feel sorry for characters who are suffering, yet this very suffering is necessary if the novel is to continue. Indeed, it creates the incentive to carry on reading and increases the reader's interest and involvement in the novel. Thus the character's misfortune and suffering and its continuance are necessary for the artistic pleasure both writer and reader derive from the novel. In the slightly ironical tone of 'alas, all this was not to be' there is an awareness that writer and reader are complicit: as human beings with moral sensibility they cannot help but regret the misfortune of the characters, but as enthusiasts for the novel as a literary form they must relish it because it allows the novel to continue and adds to its interest. Thus, paradoxically, the reader's moral relation to the content of the novel is both reinforced and undercut at the same time.

In the final paragraph contact seems to take place with Harding's kiss and blessing, which has religious as well as personal significance, but this outward contact only highlights the mental division between them, which undermines any real spiritual communion. The shift from one character's mind to another, which Trollope's form of narration is particularly well designed to capture, has thus demonstrated how human beings' different points of view inevitably create barriers to the mutual understanding which is necessary for successful human relations.

6 CRITICAL RECEPTION

6.1 CONTEMPORARY AND NINETEENTH-CENTURY VIEWS

Barchester Towers was fairly well received by contemporary reviewers in 1857. Many of their comments are still of considerable interest. The reviewer in the *Examiner*, for example, drew a comparison with Sterne's *Tristram Shandy*: 'it does not depend only on story for its interest; the careful writing, the good humour with a tendency often to be Shandean in its expression, and the sense and right feeling with which the way is threaded among questions of high church and low church, are very noticeable'. The *Spectator* made the following criticism of the characterisation: 'His characters are frequently rather abstractions of qualities than actual persons. They are rather the *made* results of skill and thought than the spontaneous productions of genius operating instinctively.' The review in the *Leader* thought the satire on the low church unfair, but argued that this was atoned for by the power of the writing, while the *Athenaeum* thought Trollope stronger on character than action and took the view that Slope was 'the Low Church personified'.

The review in the *Saturday Review* was particularly interesting. It thought the book 'very clever' and went on: 'Indeed it is, if anything, too clever, and the whole story is rather too much a series of brilliant but disjointed sketches.' It made a general comment on Trollope that shows particular insight:

He possesses an especial talent for drawing what may be called the second-class of good people – characters not noble, superior, or perfect, after the standard of human perfection, but still good and honest, with a fundamental basis of sincerity, kindliness, and religious principle, yet with a considerable proneness to temptation, and a strong consciousness that they live, and like to live, in a struggling, party-giving, comfort-seeking world.

The Times stressed the novelty of the novel's setting and the freshness of the subject and wondered 'that more has not long ago been made of such promising materials', while the *Westminster Review* praised it 'as decidedly the cleverest novel of the season', though it found Trollope 'wanting in certain of the higher elements that make a great novelist'.

One of the major nineteenth-century essays on Trollope is Henry James's essay of 1888 in *Partial Portraits*. Though critical of the narrator's 'suicidal satisfaction' in informing the reader of the novel's fictionality, he nevertheless considered it one of Trollope's best novels. It possessed 'an almost Thackerayan richness', the characters were striking, and 'the idea of transporting the Signora Vesey-Neroni into a cathedral-town was an inspiration'. Frederic Harrison, writing in 1895, also considered it one of Trollope's main achievements because it was among those of his novels which have two particular merits: 'graceful, truthful, subtle observation of contemporary types, clothed in a style of transparent ease', and the reproduction for the future of 'certain phases of life in the nineteenth century in England with minute fidelity and the most literal realism'.

6.2 TWENTIETH-CENTURY CRITICISM

Trollope's reputation suffered in the late nineteenth and early twentieth century. Michael Sadleir's *Trollope: A Commentary*, first published in 1927, attempted to revive his reputation. Sadleir thought *Barchester Towers* 'a wonderful advance' over *The Warden* and pointed out that 'beneath the suavity, was always harshness'. But Sadleir did not rate it among Trollope's greatest novels. Virginia Woolf, writing in 1929, praised the novel for its realism but concluded: 'At the top of his bent Trollope is a big, if not first-rate novelist.' James and nineteenth-century critics preferred Trollope's earlier to his later novels, but some twentieth-century critics, such as A. O. J. Cockshut and Gordon N. Ray have taken the opposite view. Ray, however, calls *Barchester Towers* Trollope's *Pride and Prejudice*, but says of the early work in general:

> These early books bear the marks of their origin in the tradition of slapdash, helter-skelter narrative which dominated English fiction during the eighteen-thirties and eighteen-forties. Proportion and consistency of taste are hardly envisioned as objectives . . . For all their vigor, dash, and brilliance, these early books lack the easy narrative mastery, the nice balance of judgement, and the harmony of tone that Trollope was shortly to make a habitual part of his equipment.

But the majority of recent critics still regard it as one of Trollope's best novels. While not denying the novel's realism, they have also placed emphasis on its structure and organisation. Ruth apRoberts writes:

> Eleanor's three suitors correspond to the three church par-
> ties . . . In the sphere of the laity, it is the Thornes who stand for
> the beauty of the Old, and its absurdity too . . . Mrs Proudie's
> Reception and the Ullathorne Games are both great climaxes in
> the structure of the novel, for in each there is the maximum
> juxtaposition of incongruities.

James R. Kincaid, in his book of 1977, argues strongly that the Ullathorne chapters are the structural and moral centre of the novel:

> And all of the novel points toward the symbolic heart of this comic
> world and the structural centre of the novel in Miss Thorne's *fête
> champêtre* at Ullathorne. The party, at first seen as a monstrous
> ritual of dedication to illusion and the dead, becomes the scene for
> clarity and rejuvenation, and the Thornes, viewed initially as
> hilariously superannuated, move closer to the approved position.

Another tendency of more recent criticism has been to suggest that the novel is more radical in viewpoint than on the surface it might appear to be. Joseph Wiesenfarth, in an essay published in 1980, takes a strongly positive view of Madeline: 'Her function in the novel is to reveal hidden motives and expose hypocrisy; she works hand-in-glove with Trollope to get out the truth.' He also argues that Harding and Bertie Stanhope are 'the heroes of Trollope's imagination': 'Bertie Stanhope and Septimus Harding are heroes in *Barchester Towers* because they are essentially unambitious men. It is good to be Arabin and get Eleanor and the deanery; but it is just as good, if not better, to be Bertie and Mr Harding and refuse Eleanor and the deanery.' Coral Lansbury, in a study published in 1981, sees sex as having an important role in the novel:

> Throughout *Barchester Towers* sex is in contention with clerical
> conventions . . . Arabin is a virgin who is aroused to the mysteries
> of sex by the Signora . . . Mrs Proudie demands chaste behaviour
> from her supporters, she trumpets her horror of Signora Neroni's
> lascivious influence, yet her own victories are never won in the
> cloisters of Barchester but in the bishop's bedroom . . . Signora
> Neroni, whose every word is a tantalizing invitation is physically
> frigid: Mrs Proudie, who flinches from the very mention of sex, is a
> volcano in the bedroom, capable of reducing a man to the shard of
> his former self.

REVISION QUESTIONS

1. In what ways does the novel exploit the incongruity between the church as a spiritual entity and its involvement with such 'worldly' matters as politics and power?
2. Can the novel be defended against the view that it is an unfair satire on the low church?
3. What factors allow the women characters to exercise such power and influence over men?
4. Discuss the role of the Stanhope family and/or the Thornes in the structure of the novel.
5. In what respects do the main characters represent significant aspects of Victorian life?
6. Henry James believed the narrator's repeated disclosure that the novel was a fiction was inartistic and undermined its credibility. Can the novel be defended against this view?
7. Does Trollope succeed in welding the different spheres of the novel and its various plots into a coherent structure? If so, how is this achieved?
8. What features of the novel are most interesting from a psychological point of view?
9. Are the qualities associated with Mr Harding the main positive element in the novel, as most critics believe? Do they have any drawbacks or disadvantages?
10. What are the major comic devices of the novel?
11. 'It is astonishing how much difference the point of view makes in the aspect of all we look at!' (Chapter 24). Does this comment by the narrator have wider significance in the novel?
12. What function do the epic parallels and the use of language associated with epic poetry serve in the novel?

FURTHER READING

Texts

The most useful edition of *Barchester Towers*, because of the thoroughness of its annotation and the interest of its introduction, is that published by Penguin Books, Harmondsworth, 1983, edited by Robin Gilmour. Other paperback editions with less full annotation can be found in World's Classics, published by Oxford University Press, 1980, and in Pan Books, London, 1980.

Biography and letters

Trollope's *Autobiography* (1883) is of considerable interest. There is a modern biography by James Pope-Hennessy, *Anthony Trollope* (London: Cape, 1971), and Trollope's letters have been edited by N. John Hall (Stanford University Press, 1983).

General criticism

Ruth apRoberts, *The Moral Trollope* (Athens, Ohio: Ohio University Press, 1971).
John W. Clark, *The Language and Style of Anthony Trollope* (London: Andre Deutsch, 1975).
A. O. J. Cockshut, *Anthony Trollope: A Critical Study* (London: Collins, 1955).
Robin Gilmour, *The Idea of the Gentleman in the Victorian Novel* (London: Allen & Unwin, 1981).
N. John Hall, *The Trollope Critics* (London: Macmillan, 1981). Contains criticism by Henry James, Frederic Harrison, Lord David Cecil, Gordon N. Ray, among others.
J. Hillis Miller, *The Form of Victorian Fiction* (Notre Dame, Indiana: Univesity of Notre Dame Press, 1968).
Michael Sadleir, *Trollope: A Commentary* (London: Constable, 1927).

David Skilton, *Anthony Trollope and his Contemporaries* (London: Longman, 1972).
Donald Smalley (ed.), *Anthony Trollope: The Critical Heritage* (London: Routledge & Kegan Paul, 1969). Contains contemporary reviews of *Barchester Towers*.
J. A. Sutherland, *Victorian Novelists and Publishers* (London: Athlone Press, 1976).

Detailed criticism of *Barchester Towers*

Tony Bareham (ed.), *Anthony Trollope* (London: Vision, 1980). Contains an interesting essay by Joseph Wiesenfarth.
Tony Bareham, (ed.), *Trollope's Barsetshire Novels: A Casebook* (London: Macmillan, 1983). Contains a number of useful essays, especially one by William Cadbury.
P. D. Edwards, *Anthony Trollope: His Art and Scope* (Brighton: Harvester Press, 1978).
U. C. Knoepflmacher, *Laughter and Despair: Readings in Ten Novels of the Victorian Period* (Berkeley: University of California Press, 1968).
James R. Kincaid, *The Novels of Anthony Trollope* (Oxford: Clarendon Press, 1977).
Coral Lansbury, *The Reasonable Man: Trollope's Legal Fiction* (Princeton, New Jersey: Princeton University Press, 1981).
Robert Polhemus, *The Changing World of Anthony Trollope* (Berkeley: University of California Press, 1968).
W. David Shaw, 'Moral Drama in *Barchester Towers*', *Nineteenth-Century Fiction*, 19 (1964), pp. 45–54.